Greatest Football Games *of All Time*

Greatest
FOOTBALL GAMES
of All Time

by Hank Hersch

SPORTS ILLUSTRATED is a
registered trademark of Time Inc.

ISBN 1-883013-26-7
Manufactured in the United States of America
First printing 1997

Sports Illustrated Director of Development: STANLEY WEIL

GREATEST FOOTBALL GAMES OF ALL TIME
Project Director: MORIN BISHOP
  Senior Editors: JOHN BOLSTER, SALLY GUARD, EVE PETERSON
  Reporters: LAUREN CARDONSKY, JESSICA GOLDSTEIN
  Photography Editors: JOHN S. BLACKMAR, TED MENZIES
Designers: BARBARA CHILENSKAS, JIA BAEK

GREATEST FOOTBALL GAMES OF ALL TIME was prepared by
Bishop Books, Inc.
611 Broadway
New York, New York 10012

Cover photograph (Joe Namath):
WALTER IOOSS JR.

TIME INC. HOME ENTERTAINMENT
Managing Director: DAVID GITOW
Director, Continuities and Single Sales: DAVID ARFINE
Director, Continuities and Retention: MICHAEL BARRETT
Director, New Products: ALICIA LONGOBARDO
Product Managers: CHRISTOPHER BERZOLLA, ROBERT FOX,
STACY HIRSCHBERG, MICHAEL HOLAHAN, AMY JACOBSSON,
JENNIFER MCLYMAN, DAN MELORE
Manager, Retail and New Markets: THOMAS MIFSUD
Associate Product Managers: LOUISA BARTLE, ALISON
EHRMANN, NANCY LONDON, DAWN WELAND
Assistant Product Managers: MEREDITH SHELLEY, BETTY SU
Editorial Operations Director: JOHN CALVANO
Fulfillment Director: MICHELLE GUDEMA
Financial Director: TRICIA GRIFFIN
Associate Financial Manager: AMY MASELLI
Marketing Assistant: SARAH HOLMES

CONSUMER MARKETING DIVISION
Production Director: JOHN E. TIGHE
Book Production Manager: DONNA MIANO-FERRARA
Assistant Book Production Manager: JESSICA MCGRATH

Special thanks to: JOSEPH NAPOLITANO

CONTENTS

INTRODUCTION

Joe Namath stars in two of our games, once as
a loser, and once, more memorably, as a winner.

More than 10,000 NFL games have been played since the founding
of the league in 1920. While it is possible to rank them in order of
greatness, that would require a consensus on what that term means.
Sure, we all know a great game when we see it. Indelible images
form in the mind's eye; the pulse quickens as the clock ticks; each
pivotal play becomes a matter of pure—often endless—analysis and
debate and joy. It is in the hope of seeing this sort of exhilarating
competition that we flip on the tube on a Sunday afternoon and half-
watch, until the action seizes our attention and won't let go.

Such games can't be reduced to a simple list. One that was ripe
with edge-of-the-seat theatrics (such as the San Diego Chargers'
overtime conquest of the Miami Dolphins in 1982) might lack the
historical impact of another that was a blowout (such as the Green

**Both of our great games featuring Green Bay were wins for the Packers, due in no
small measure to their defense and the intimidating Ray Nitschke (right, 66).**

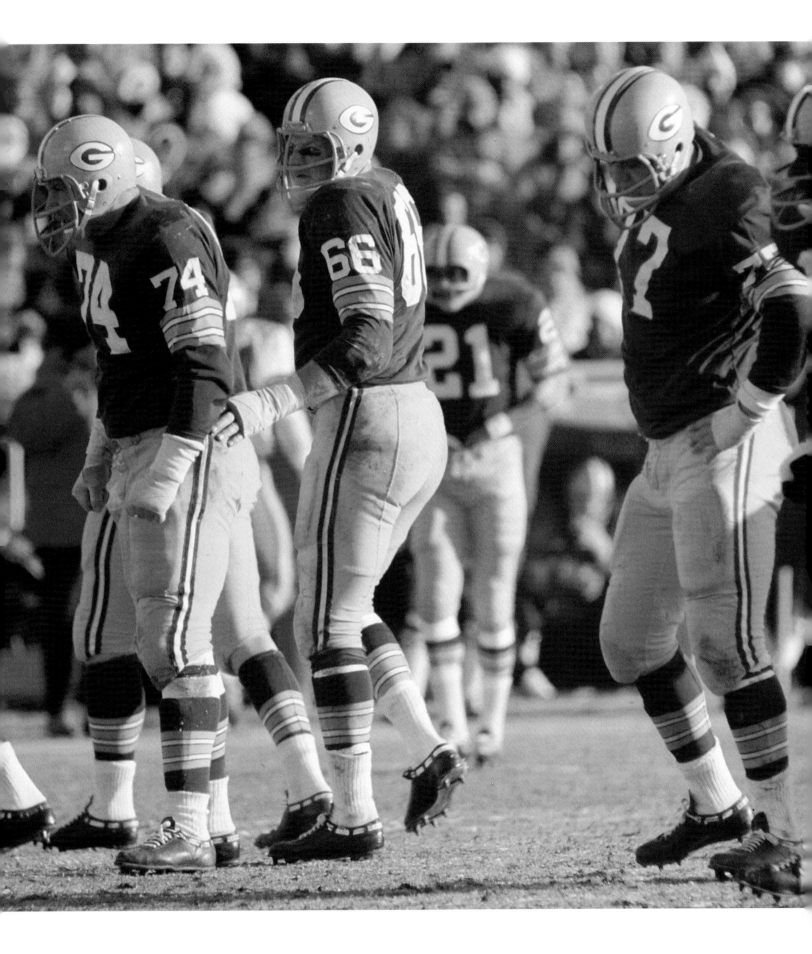

John Elway led the Denver Broncos on an unforget-
table drive that still haunts the Cleveland faithful.

Bay Packers' victory over the Kansas City Chiefs in Super Bowl I).
One that was prized for the dazzling output of a single player (see
Gale Sayers's six-touchdown performance, 1965) might not have the
surprise ending that adds an enduring moniker to the football lexicon
(see the Immaculate Reception, 1972). One that had almost every
conceivable element of excitement but took place before the advent
of television (the 1933 championship game) might not be the equal
to one witnessed by tens of millions (the championship game of '58).

   With these disparities in mind, we have organized this book in a
non-hierarchical way. We have taken what we believe to be the vari-
ous components of a great game, set them out as headings and sorted
our entries accordingly. The results are, we hope, revealing.

John Taylor caught the pass from Joe Montana that capped
San Francisco's dramatic come-from-behind victory in Super Bowl XXIII.

Dan Fouts was heroic in San Diego's 1982 win over Miami, throwing for 433 yards.

Names such as Halas and Lombardi and Brown dominate the section on Big Games. Of our six One-Man Game stories, five feature Hall of Famers; the other a Pittsburgh Steelers wide receiver who has been knocking on the door at Canton for years, Lynn Swann. The Comebacks chapter twice zeroes in on one of the league's most gifted improvisers, Dallas Cowboys quarterback Roger Staubach. Field-goal kickers, usually the littlest guys on the field, loom largest during the last, worrisome moments in Nail-Biters. Under the heading of Fantastic Finishes are two drives, each of which covered a lot of distance, but meant wholly different—yet still fantastic— things to people in different places.

And it is no surprise that lesser-known troops such as Tony Guillory, Mel Hein and Tom (the Bomb) Tracy emerge from the crucible of these memorable battles. For they too are players, and in a great game, above all, the play's the thing.

Though the games vary, in the end all winning teams express their joy in much the same way the Redskins did after their win over the Raiders in 1983 (right).

10

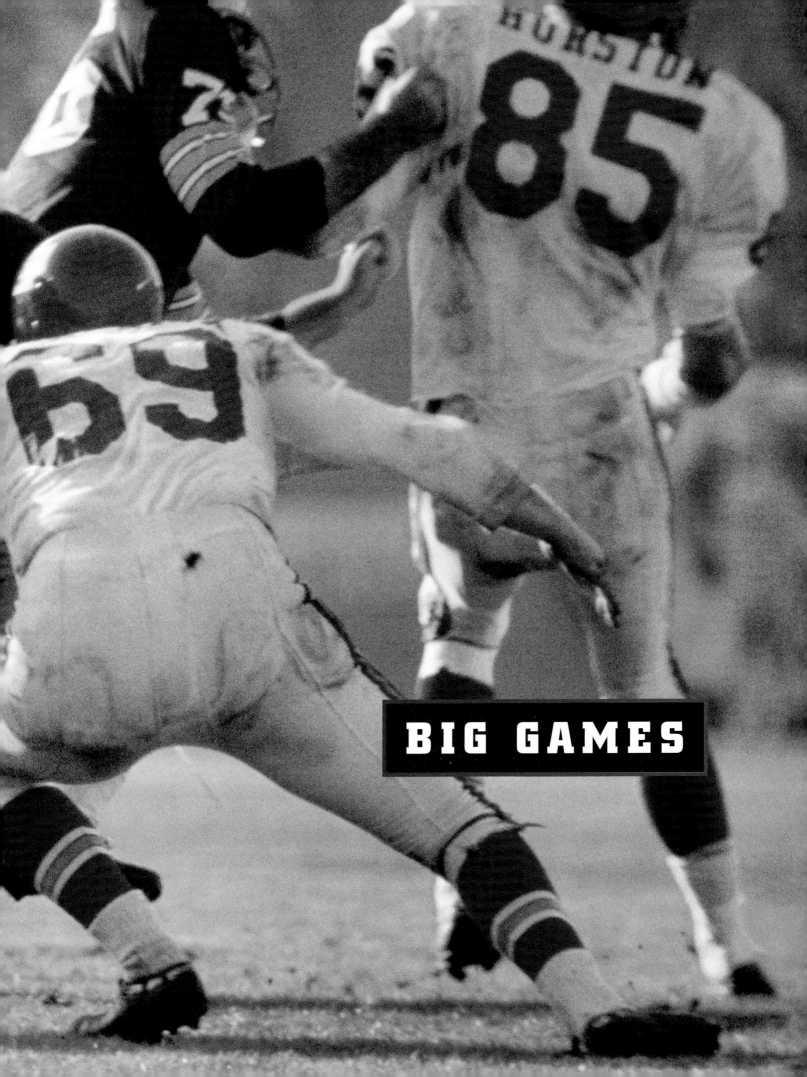

BIG GAMES

A pair of quarterback's backs: Joe Namath (above) guaranteed victory, then delivered; Bart Starr (right) was the epitome of cool in the Packers' win in Super Bowl I.

OVERVIEW

The history of pro football is marked by showdowns in which a lot was on the line—a playoff spot, a conference title, the pride of an entire league. It is to win these games that grown men (growing bigger by the year) practice twice a day in the summer heat, charge onto the field despite enduring absurd amounts of pain and eagerly do violence unto their opponents. Each victory when the stakes are high is a sweet, inalienable payoff for untold hours of sacrifice. But only a handful of the dozens and dozens of big games have changed the landscape of the sport.

Let's take it from the top—the first NFL championship matchup, in 1932. The staging of the game wasn't immediately recognized as a watershed moment, perhaps because it was played in a hockey arena layered with the droppings of circus elephants that had recently passed through. But after watching the drama at Chicago Stadium, the league's higher-ups saw the value in having the season reach a crescendo.

That sense was reinforced the following year, outdoors, when the Chicago Bears and New York Giants tried every trick in the book—and a few that weren't— to gain victory. Many of the game's principals called it the greatest game ever played, but only the immensity of the stakes made it great. Some 25 years later the Baltimore Colts and New York Giants vied for the same stakes but drove the excitement level even higher. They played into sudden-death overtime, transfixing the now TV-happy nation. Many of those who bore witness would call *it* the greatest game ever played.

The NFL has become the nation's preeminent sporting enterprise by absorbing some upstart

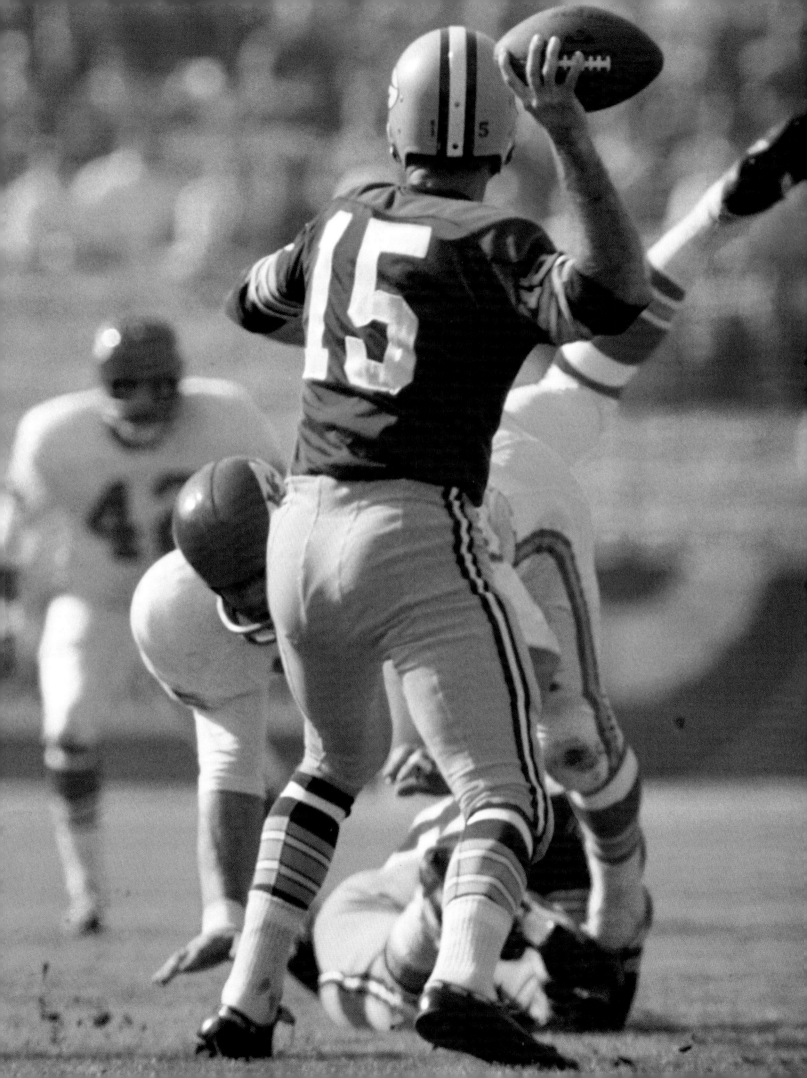

Max McGee (left) fought off a hangover, then went out and caught seven passes against the Chiefs in Super Bowl I; for Don Shula (above, right), the loss in Super Bowl III was just the first of six trips to the biggest game of them all.

leagues and grinding others into submisson. After World War II the league faced a challenge from the All-America Football Conference. Slowly, surely, the NFL asserted its superiority, forcing the bulk of the AAFC to fold and allowing three of its eight members entry. To teach the newcomers a lesson, the NFL arranged for its 1949 titlist, the Philadelphia Eagles, to meet the AAFC's reigning champ, the Cleveland Browns in the season opener. But it was the NFL that was taught a lesson: Beware of whom you merge with.

On Jan. 15, 1967, that lesson still must have been on the league owners' minds. The NFL's Green Bay Packers met the AFL's Kansas City Chiefs at Los Angeles Memorial Coliseum in a much-ballyhooed event soon to be called the Super Bowl. Once again, the idea was to prove the senior circuit's superiority, but, playing to a crowd of 60 million curious TV viewers, the Chiefs lifted the AFL's visibility to unmatched heights. Afterward, the NFL was uncertain which tack to take in dealing with its newest rival. Two years later, in Super Bowl III, the New York Jets would leave the league little choice.

17

PACKERS / CHIEFS

35 / 10

January 15, 1967

The first Super Bowl had saturation coverage: NBC and CBS paid $1 million each for the rights to broadcast the game. It had riches: Those fees, plus $750,000 in gate receipts at the Los Angeles Memorial Coliseum, made it the most lucrative sports event ever held in the United States. It had bombast: Kansas City cornerback Fred (the Hammer) Williamson vowed time and again to add some Green Bay headgear to the trove of 30 helmets he had supposedly cracked. It had what dozens of Super Bowls to follow would have as well: a lopsided final score.

But unlike the others, this one changed the landscape of pro football. By surviving and continuing to pluck talented college players the seven-year-old AFL had goaded the 48-year-old NFL into sanctioning this season-ending matchup, and when the Chiefs charged onto the sun-splashed field before 63,036 spectators to face Vince Lombardi's nonpareil Packers, the upstart league gained legitimacy that it never could have otherwise. While most pro football fans considered the Super Bowl an anticlimax to the Green Bay-Dallas NFL title tilt a fortnight earlier, the possibility of an upset was enough to tantalize 60 million TV viewers, many of whom would never have trifled with the AFL under normal circumstances.

The Packers, favored by 13 points, felt the pressure. "We've just beaten Dallas for our second straight championship," safety Tom Brown said before the game. "But if we lose this game, people will remember us as the NFL team that lost to Kansas City in the first game played between the two leagues." Lombardi had planned to avoid arriving in the cozy California climate until just before the kickoff, but NFL commissioner Pete Rozelle insisted he bring the team out a week early to promote the game. The

McGee came off the shady end of the bench to grab seven passes for 138 yards and a pair of touchdowns.

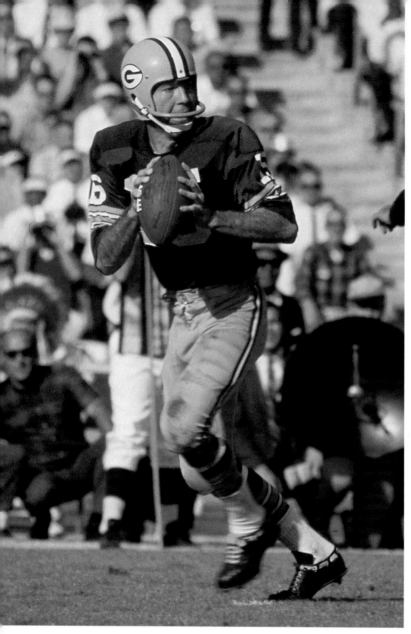

The precise Starr threw for 250 yards while extending his streak of passes without an interception to 173.

through the establishment. In the press box, NFL troubleshooter Buddy Young fretted. "Old age and heat are gonna get the Packers in the second half," he said. "The Chiefs are a mighty good football team."

In the locker room Lombardi made a blunt appeal for the restoration of order in the pro football ranks. "Are you the world champion Green Bay Packers?" he asked his players. "Get on the field and give me your answer."

They did. Never a fan of gimmickry, Lombardi had opted to rush only his front four in the first half. In the second, he came out blitzing. With the Chiefs facing third down on their own 45, outside linebackers Lee Roy Caffey and Dave Robinson crashed through the line, zipping up quarterback Len Dawson's futuristic pocket. His pass was tipped by tackle Henry Jordan and swiped by defensive back Willie Wood, who returned the ball to the five. On the next play running back Elijah Pitts scored to make it 21–10, and the rout was on.

Garrett wound up rushing for only 17 yards. Dawson completed only five of 12 passes for 59 after halftime. Williamson was carried off the field in the fourth quarter with a broken arm. "It's impossible for me to believe that those balding old men on the Packers could have handled us with such ridiculous ease," said Kansas City running back Jerry Mays. "We mangled 'em a little bit," acknowledged Green Bay fullback Jim Taylor.

Unerring Packer quarterback Bart Starr earned the first Super Bowl MVP award. Against a "stack" defense designed to stop the run, he connected on 16 of 23 throws for 250 yards using the NFL ball and ran his streak of passes without a pickoff to 173. Starr's primary target was 34-year-old end Max McGee, who had made just four receptions during the season but was summoned off the bench when Boyd Dowler was injured in the Pack's first series. To be more specific, McGee was summoned off the *shady end* of the bench, where he had been nursing a hangover. He finished with seven catches for 138 yards, including two TD grabs.

In the steamy Packer dressing room after the game, McGee announced his retirement while Lombardi dismissed the Chiefs as a swift, but not particularly tough team, by the standards of the senior circuit. While making his remarks he slammed a football from hand to hand. "The boys gave me a game ball," Lombardi said proudly. "An NFL ball."

Pack relented, but practiced in relative seclusion, 90 miles north of the Coliseum, in Santa Barbara, where Lombardi decreed that plays be run in the least scenic direction. "We're not here to look at the mountains,"he barked.

Though he would not admit having deigned to watch an AFL game, Lombardi knew he would have to contend with the "moving pocket" in Kansas City coach Hank Stram's "offense of the future." Stram believed his speedy attack, fueled by halfback Mike Garrett, could outflank the Pack. And for the first half, in the L.A.'s 75-degree weather, it did.

Though they trailed 14–10, the Chiefs used the narrower, more passing-friendly AFL ball on their possessions to outgain Green Bay 181 yards to 164, sending a ripple of fear

The normally prolific Dawson was held to just five completions and 59 passing yards in the second half.

When commissioner Pete Rozelle announced the AFL–NFL merger agreement on June 8, 1966, hostilities between the two leagues did not cease, but merely shifted in focus. They had competed feverishly over the past six years for players, fans and TV revenues and now, Rozelle declared, they would compete on the football field in a year-end championship. Regular-season play would follow in 1970. But the first two

Super Bowls ended in lopsided defeats for the AFL, and doubts surfaced about the outlaw league's ability to compete. One newspaper head-

AFTERMATH

line read, LOMBARDI SAYS AFL INFERIOR. That was the clipping Johnny Sample of the New York Jets produced the following year, when the AFL champions delivered on Joe Namath's infa-

mous guarantee to beat the heavily-favored Colts in Super Bowl III. No one could doubt the AFL's equality now, but difficulties over the draft and divisional realignment persisted. Finally, Rozelle locked all 26 owners in a room and ordered them to jot down their alignment proposals on scraps of paper. He placed these in a vase and asked his secretary to draw one. With that, the NFL entered the most prosperous era in its history.

New York Jets quarterback Joe Namath said he hosted two types of events at his penthouse apartment on Manhattan's Upper East Side: get-togethers, (guys coming over to eat steaks and play cards), and parties (get-togethers that included women). The centerpiece of the place was a white llama-skin rug that, like Broadway Joe's white cleats, long hair and Fu Manchu mustache—which he refused to shave even for $10,000—had come to represent his estimable sense of cool. Fans of a more strait-laced order, of course, seized upon those symbols in dismissing Namath as nothing more than a passing fancy.

At an awards ceremony four days before a get-together called Super Bowl III, the 25-year-old Namath guaranteed that the AFL's Jets, a 17-point underdog, would beat the NFL's Colts. Three days later he reaffirmed that vow while lounging poolside in his swim trunks at a Miami hotel. "We're a better team than Baltimore," he told the clutch of reporters hovering around his chaise longue.

Namath's utterance had about as much heft as a pickup line. By game time the bookies had fattened the spread to 19½. Colts owner Carroll Rosenbloom was gracious enough to extend an invitation to his postgame victory gala to Weeb Ewbank, the New York coach.

The Colts, after all, were fresh off a 34–0 rout of Cleveland that had run their record over the last two years to 28–2. A fearsome blitz had helped earn their defense billing as one of the best of all time. The Jets, on the other hand, were limping in on Namath's balky knees and saddled with both an ordinary D and the sad legacy of their league. In the first two Super Bowls, the tackle-to-tackle NFL had trampled the bombs-away AFL by a combined score of 68–24. "Namath plays his first pro

Namath's mighty right arm produced 206 passing yards en route to the Jets' shocking defeat of the heavily favored Colts.

football game today," one coach cracked before the kickoff.

But Namath was not being flip or quixotic in making his guarantee. He sincerely believed in New York's talent, and had real doubts about the speed of Baltimore's secondary and the skill of opposing quarterback Earl Morrall, who he said would be a third-stringer on the Jets. As he prepared to take the field before the start of the game, Namath turned to a teammate in the locker room. "I feel loose, real loose," he said. "My arm is so loose I think it's gonna fall off."

Ewbank had warned Namath not to run any sweeps out of respect for the fleet Colts linebackers. On the Jets' second play, Namath called an audible that sent fullback Matt Snell on a sweep around the left end for a first down. Early in the second quarter Broadway Joe piloted the Jets 80 yards on 12 plays to take a 7–0 lead. Snell roared in on, yes,

a four-yard sweep. Snell would finish with 121 tough yards on 30 carries. "He's a great runner," said Jets offensive tackle Winston Hill. "The mediocre backs come back to the huddle and cry if they didn't get a hole big enough to back a truck through. Snell doesn't ask for much room."

To blunt the Baltimore offense Ewbank added a linebacker to make a five-man front. The Colts were able to drive against it, but only up to a point—one at which they self-destructed. Time and again New York swiped Colts passes: one on the goal line, one in the end zone, one on the two-yard line and a fourth that was even more devastating. With the ball on the Jets' 41 late in the second quarter, Morrall handed off to Tom Matte, who threw a lateral back to Morrall. Near the goal line, receiver Jimmy Orr stood uncovered. To get noticed, "I did everything but shoot up a flare,"

The Jets' surprisingly successful running game was spearheaded by Matt Snell, who shredded the Colts for 121 yards on 30 carries.

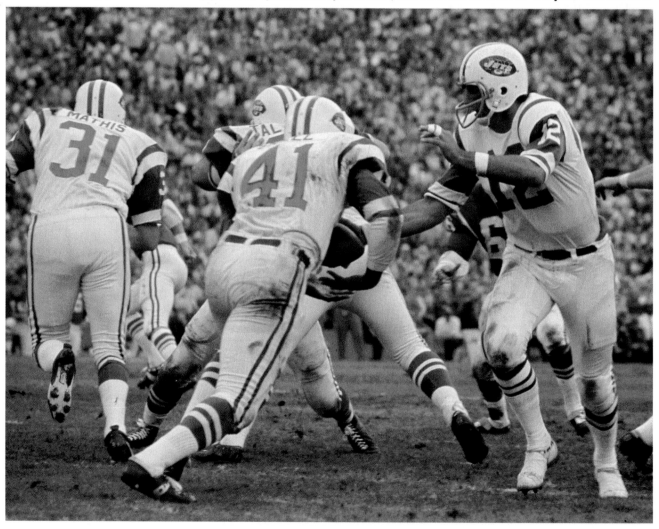

Orr said. Morrall missed him. He tried to hit fullback Jerry Hill instead, and Jim Hudson stepped in to make the pick. "I'm just a lineman, but I looked up and saw Orr open," Colts center Bill Curry said. "I don't know what happened."

With three minutes to go in the third quarter, Baltimore coach Don Shula replaced Morrall with his 36-year-old backup. But even Johnny Unitas, who had salvaged win after win for Ewbank in his eight years as Baltimore's coach, had trouble finding the end zone. The Colts' only score came with 3:19 to play and the Jets up 16–0 after Jim Turner's third field goal.

Namath charged off the field waving the index finger of the right hand that had whipped the mighty Colts. Damn the credibility gap, and up the establishment: By completing 17 of 28 passes for 206 yards and no interceptions, he had upheld his promise, vindicated the AFL and made a planned merger between the two leagues seem feasible.

In the Jets triumphant locker room, a reporter asked Namath to describe his emotions. "That would take too much time and too much thinking," Namath said. "I'd rather just enjoy it."

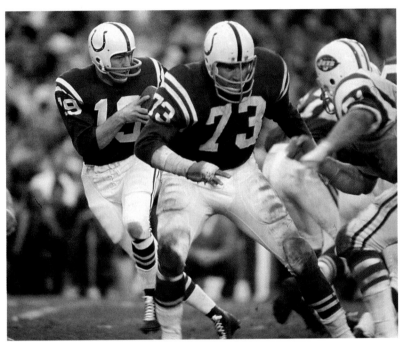 

As Baltimore's former head coach, Ewbank (right) had seen Unitas (19) manufacture multiple miracles; this time the magic was absent.

Namath is a superb quarterback who in the Super Bowl last week proved that his talent is as big as his mouth—which makes it a very big talent, indeed. He went from Broadway Joe to Super Joe on a cloud-covered afternoon in Miami, whipping the Baltimore Colts, champions of the National Football League, 16–7 in the process.

Almost no one thought the New York Jets could penetrate the fine Baltimore defense, but Namath was sure of it and said so.... It was called loudmouthing, bragging, but as it turned out, Super Joe told it

the way it was. In a surpassing display of passing accuracy and mental agility, he picked the Colt defense apart. Then, with a comfortable 16–0 lead, he prudently relied upon a surprisingly strong running game through most of the fourth quarter to protect that lead. He read the puzzling Colt defenses as easily as if they had been printed in comic books, and the Colt blitz, a fearsome thing during the regular NFL season, only provided Namath with the opportunity to complete key passes.

—Tex Maule
January 20, 1969

A historic first on a hallowed field. Two lineups blessed with 15 future Hall of Famers. A controversial call. A dubious coaching decision. A goal-line stand. A desperate drive. More turning points than the Appalachian Trail. Rampant heroism. Sudden death. Maiden victory. "The greatest game I've ever seen," according to the league's commissioner, Bert Bell.

There were 6,000 empty seats that damp, gray day at Yankee Stadium, prompting a TV blackout in the New York area. Thus, the most indelible impression millions had of Colts fullback Alan (the Horse) Ameche didn't come at 4:51 p.m., when he blasted into the end zone and through the wearied hearts of the Giants to punctuate the first overtime championship game in the NFL's 38-year history. It came hours later, when he stood up in the audience on *The Ed Sullivan Show* and was recognized by the host. Ameche pocketed $500 for that appearance, which, with his winner's share for helping Baltimore reap its first title, brought his payday to $5,218.77.

Quarterback Johnny Unitas had turned down $750 to make the same beauty-pageant wave. Had Ameche passed on appearing as well, Sullivan would have had numerous other worthy Colts to entice. There was left end Raymond Berry, who snagged a championship-record 12 passes for 178 yards, including three for 62 yards on the tying march which began with 1:56 left in regulation. There was coach Weeb Ewbank, who had his team prepared (having given his players maps that highlighted the spoft spots on the field) and fired up (by a sideline swing he took at New York linebacker Sam Huff for a dirty play).

There was hulking defensive end Gino Marchetti, who,

Ameche's game-winning score in overtime yielded a first NFL title for Baltimore and an appearance on *Ed Sullivan* for him.

With seven seconds left in regulation, Myrha's 20-yarder went up into the twilight and through the uprights for the game-tying score.

before breaking both bones in his lower right leg in the fourth quarter, spearheaded a defense that twice forced the Giants to punt when one first down would have sealed their fourth championship. Ewbank awarded Marchetti the game ball. "Hell, I oughta cut this thing up in 50 pieces," Marchetti said. "I never saw a game that had so much. So many players who made such big plays."

And not just Colts. Consider: After completing 26 of 40 passes for 349 yards and one touchdown—delivering a scoring strike in his 26th straight game—Unitas was named the game's MVP and received a Corvette. When the initial vote was taken with five minutes to play in the fourth quarter, though, Giants quarterback Charlie Conerly, a 37-year-old backup, was to have received the title and the wheels.

Before a crowd of 64,185 Conerly relieved Don Heinrich and rallied the Giants from a 14–3 deficit created by

New York halfback Frank Gifford's two first-half fumbles. Only a brilliant goal-line stand in the third quarter, climaxed by linebacker Cliff Livingston's stuffing of Ameche on fourth-and-one, prevented the game from getting out of reach. Taking over then on downs, Conerly responded with a 95-yard, five-play blitz to cut the lead to 14–10. Then, 53 seconds into the fourth quarter, Gifford redeemed himself with a 15-yard touchdown catch from Conerly, carrying cornerback Milt Davis the final five yards to make it 17–14, Giants.

New York had a chance to seal the win with time running out. Gifford took Conerly's third-down handoff on the Giants' 40, needing only four yards to get a fresh series of downs. But Marchetti eluded Bob Schnelker's block and got his mitts on Gifford. In the ensuing pileup Marchetti's right tibia and fibula snapped. "It sounded like a gunshot," said Colts defensive tackle Art Donovan. In the confusion the referee, who waited to spot the ball until after Marchetti had been carried off the field, may have erred in his placement.

"He was too concerned about Marchetti," said New York wide receiver Kyle Rote. "I saw him pick it up at his front foot and put it down where his back foot was." A measurement indicated that the Giants were five inches short. "I made that first down," Gifford said. "I know I did."

New York coach Jim Lee Howell chose not to gamble on fourth down, relying instead on punter Don Chandler and a defense that one week before had held Cleveland great Jim Brown to a mere eight rushing yards. Though many would question Howell's choice later, when Chandler's punt was fair-caught at the Baltimore 14 with 1:56 to play, it seemed a wise maneuver. "When we got in the huddle, I looked down the field," Berry said. "The goal posts looked like they were in Baltimore."

The sidelines pinched against him, Unitas threw down the middle of the field. He connected with Lenny Moore for 11 yards, then with Berry for 25, 15 and 22. With seven seconds left, Steve Myrha, who had missed two field goals earlier, nailed a 20-yarder to tie the score.

Unitas's resourcefulness, his genius, was even more evi-

Berry made acrobatic grabs all day, catching a championship-record 12 passes for 178 yards.

dent in overtime. After the Giants won the toss, received the ball, stalled and punted, he took over on his own 20 and clicked off a pair of first downs. Faced with a third-and-15, Unitas pitched a 21-yard strike to Berry that moved Baltimore to New York's 43. On the next play he audibled a trap that sprang Ameche for 23 yards. Five plays later, Ameche barreled over right tackle.

It was 4:51 pm, and dusk had descended on Yankee Stadium. "When you can't hold them, you can't win," Howell said afterward. "They deserved it and we have no alibis."

His name suggests a hero out of the *Chip Hilton* series for young readers: Johnny Unitas. Johnny Unite Us. The hero who never fails to lead his team to victory in the final seconds. The unflappable Unitas did precisely that many times, most famously on December 28, 1958. But the beginning of his career was hardly the stuff of storybooks. Drafted by the Pittsburgh Steelers in the ninth round

SPOTLIGHT

out of the University of Louisville in 1955, Unitas was unceremoniously dumped before the end of training camp. He got a second chance in '56 when the Baltimore Colts lost their backup quarterback and claimed Unitas on waivers. He made the team, warming the bench behind starter

George Shaw, the previous season's rookie sensation. Shaw suffered a knee injury in October, however, and the Colts were forced to turn to their castoff backup. Little did they know they were launching an 18-year, Hall-of-Fame career. Unitas would lead Baltimore to NFL titles in 1958 and '59, and accumulate 40,239 career passing yards while establishing himself as one of the very best in the clutch.

BROWNS / EAGLES

September 16, 1950

At its own peril, the established order has forever underestimated revolutionaries. Hence the NFL's disdain for the Cleveland Browns.

True, they had gone 47-4-3 in four seasons in the All-America Football Conference and swept its championship games. But the throne of the AAFC was not exactly exalted. The league had lost $11 million over that quadrennium and only the Baltimore Colts, the San Francisco 49ers and the Browns were deemed stable and solvent enough to join the NFL when the two leagues merged after the 1949 season. Said Washington Redskins owner George Preston Marshall, wrapped in his trademark coonskin coat and gazing down the barrel of his patrician nose, "The worst team in our league could beat the best team in theirs."

To make that superiority incontrovertibly clear, commissioner Bert Bell scheduled the Browns to kick off the 1950 campaign on a Saturday night, the day before the rest of the league began play. Their opponent: the NFL's reigning champion Eagles, at Philadelphia's Municipal Stadium. Philly owner James Clark, who had bought the team once owned by Bell, was an adamant opponent of the merger, and coach Earle (Greasy) Neale potshotted Cleveland's coach as a sideline sap better suited to coaching basketball. "All he does is put the ball up in the air," Neale said.

Neale had no idea, of course, that he was peremptorily dismissing the visionary father of modern pro football, the man who would introduce, among other staples of the game, precision pass routes, messenger guards to shuttle in plays from the sidelines, a grading system for players, the notion of a staff of full-time assistant coaches and the use of the 40-yard dash to gauge players' speed. But then, it was easy for an established coach in an established league to underestimate brown-suited Paul Brown.

Just one of several fleet Cleveland receivers, the aptly named Speedie caught seven passes for 109 yards and a TD.

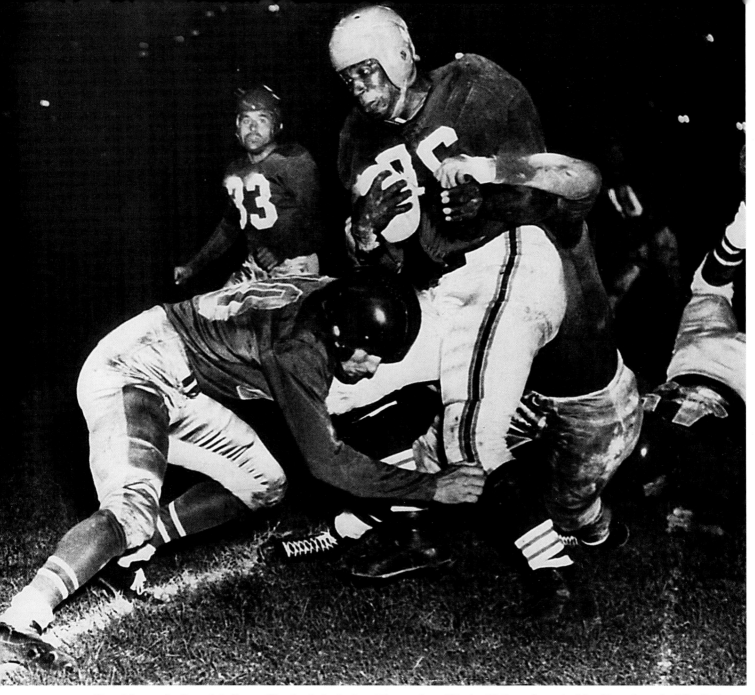

Though known for its aerial offense, Cleveland also featured the running of Marion Motley, who rushed for 48 yards against the Eagles.

As Cleveland lineman Lin Houston said of his team's AAFC tenure, "For four years, we had put up with being called a high school team with a high school coach."

The 42-year-old Brown had indeed built his reputation as a high school coach in Ohio, where over nine seasons he went 81-7-2 before joining Ohio State, which he guided to the 1942 national championship. When Cleveland hired him in '45, he was on leave from the Buckeyes and serving as a lieutenant in the Navy. The AAFC started play after World War II, and Brown quickly distinguished himself as an iconoclast. He refused to support a "no raiding" pact with the NFL and railed against a "gentleman's agreement" to keep black players out of the new league.

Led by quarterback Otto Graham, Brown's offense might have seemed amateurish to Neale. But anyone wondering whether Brown's teams were tough enough needed only to know his motto: Expect to win. Brown, in fact, was a buttoned-down taskmaster who inspired in his troops equal parts admiration and loathing. It was nothing for him, upon hearing the slightest snicker during a film meeting, to flick on the lights and in the instantaneous silence, bark, "Nothing funny about football."

The fun that the NFL had poked at him, the Browns and the AAFC—"four years of constant ridicule," Brown called it—did little to lighten his spirits. In preparation for his day of rebuttal, Brown scouted the Eagles in '49 and before the game left no motivational stone unturned. "Coach Brown should have been a general," said Graham. "For four years he never said a word, just kept putting that stuff on the bulletin board. We were so fired up for this, we would've played them anywhere anytime—for a keg of beer or a chocolate milk shake, it didn't matter."

While Neale nonchalantly spent one Eagles practice lying on the field eating yogurt—"This is the best team ever put together," he said. "Who is there to beat us?"—Brown worried about winding his team too tight. His pregame message was terse. "Remember, that the worst thing you can do to an opponent is beat him," Brown said. "Nothing hurts worse than losing."

A crowd of 71,237 packed the house to see the answer to what *The New York Times* called "the most repeated question in gridiron history: Can the Browns beat the Eagles in Philadelphia?" Philly jumped out to a 3–0 lead, but on Cleveland's next possession end Dub Jones ran a square out, linebacker Russ Craft bit on the fake, Graham feathered a pass downfield and Jones streaked in for a 59-yard score. Then Graham began doing just what Neale had derided. He threw to Dante Lavelli for a 26-yard TD in the second quarter and to Mac Speedie for a 12-yard score in the third. The NFL was getting its comeuppance.

Neale ditched his T-formation to little avail. Cleveland would allow just 118 yards while Graham connected on

Graham (left, with Brown) received the game's MVP trophy for his outstanding performance in the Browns' NFL debut.

21 of 38 throws for 346 yards, carving up a defense that had allowed only 11.2 points a game a season earlier. "Otto Graham may be the best quarterback who ever played the game," said Philly tackle Bucko Kilroy. Affirmed Brown, "I think today we were the best football team I've ever seen. And I've seen a lot."

It would be up to an air-traffic controller to try to restore order. As the Browns' plane taxied for departure, he snapped to the pilot: "You're cleared for takeoff. Get these goddamn Browns out of Philadelphia!"

Cleveland finished its first NFL season 10–2 and beat the New York Giants 8–3 in a playoff game to claim the Eastern Division crown. In the NFL championship game a week later, Graham threw for four touchdown passes and Lou Groza kicked a field goal with 28 seconds on the clock to give the Brown's a 30–28 win over the Los Angeles Rams. The Browns' all-star combination of visionary coaching, precision quarterbacking, Hall of Fame linemen (Frank Gatski, Mike McCormack, Bill Willis, Groza), peerless receivers (Dub Jones, Mac Speedie, Dante Lavelli), a superb pass rusher (Len Ford) and the best blocking and running back of the time (Marion Motley) took them to the championship game in each of the next five seasons. After a 24–17 title loss to the Rams in '51, followed by two consecutive title losses to the Lions, the Browns beat the Lions by 46 to win the 1954 championship game. In 1955, they beat the Rams by 24 to claim their seventh league championship title in ten professional seasons, a record unmatched by any team in football history.

AFTERMATH

BEARS / SPARTANS

As the Roman numerals affixed to the Super Bowl continue to climb, it becomes increasingly difficult to imagine that there was ever a time when the NFL season didn't end with two weeks of hype, pageantry, inane questions to 300-pound athletes and—oh, yes—a title showdown. But as the Great Depression whittled the league from 18 teams in 1922 to a mere eight a decade later, thoughts about the future were hardly so grandiose. Only in a desperation attempt to promote pro football did the league's leaders decide to stage a championship game, in 1932.

As devised by NFL president Joe Carr, the game would pit two teams with the same record against each other—which, in the end, required some fudging. The Bears and the Portsmouth (Ohio) Spartans both finished 6-1, but Chicago had six ties and Portsmouth, four. The league called the season a draw anyway, perhaps because it had already booked Chicago's Wrigley Field as the site of the title fight. In so doing the NFL would indirectly wind up with reconstructed fields, revamped offense and renewed faith among fans in the league's future. For revolutionary impact, as Bears owner George Halas put it, "I don't think anything could compare with the game between Portsmouth and the Bears in 1932."

It was not until Super Bowl XII at the Superdome in New Orleans in 1978, that the league staged its championship matchup indoors—unless of course you count this inaugural, played 46 years earlier. When the Spartans reached Chicago three days before the game, Wrigley Field was blanketed in 18 inches of snow. Halas thought quickly: The Bears had played an exhibition game two years before at Chicago Stadium, home of the hockey Blackhawks; the Salvation Army had just held a circus

Chicago Stadium was surely the strangest venue for a championship game in the history of the NFL.

there, which meant there was already a layer of dirt on the floor. The game could still be on.

Halas trucked sod into the stadium, and when it was in place, there lay a six-inch-deep field consisting of 400 tons of dirt and grass. Not that the playing surface, redolent of elephant droppings, was championship-worthy. It was 15 feet narrower than regulation size and only 80 yards long. Portsmouth coach Potsy Clark said, "The place looked square the first time I saw it."

Kickoffs were taken from the 10-yard line instead of the 40, and when a team crossed midfield it had to move back 20 yards to make the field play at 100 yards. The goal posts were moved from the end lines to the goal lines, which would become the league's standard setup the following year. And when the ball was downed within 15 yards of the sideline, instead of making the next snap occur alongside a wall, officials spotted the ball 15 yards in from the sideline. Thus, hash marks were born.

Indeed, innovation marked the game, even if it did turn out to be a pedestrian defensive struggle typical of the era. (In 1932, one out of every five games ended up deadlocked, many of them scoreless). Some 12,000 fans snuggled in to watch punts bounce off the rafters, a pass sail into the mezzanine, and each team's D rampage over the narrow field. Chicago got the first break with 11 minutes to play, when Dick Nesbitt intercepted a pass and returned it to the

In the days of two-way players, NFL teams such as the Bears (below) were much smaller than today's 45-man squads.

Grange (left) and Nagurski constituted the Bears' potent backfield.

Portsmouth 13. The Bears' star fullback, Bronko Nagurski, carried for six yards, then five, then twice for zero.

On third-and-goal from the two, Nagurski charged toward the line again. This time he stopped short, backpedaled and heaved a jump pass to his backfield mate, Red Grange, who had been left uncovered in the end zone. Clark protested Grange's TD catch: The rules prevented any forward pass from being thrown within five yards of the line of scrimmage. But referee Bobby Cahn refused to budge, and with the point after, Chicago took a 7–zip lead. (The controversy would prompt the league to change the rules the following season. From then on, forward throws from anywhere behind the line would be permitted—the first step toward the modern era of pass-happy offenses.) The Bears added a safety on a fumbled snap by Portsmouth punter Mule Wilson to seal the victory.

Because of the game's success, in 1933 the league split up its teams; the winners of the Eastern and Western Divisions would meet in the NFL Championship Game. Still, Halas had a hard time accepting the virtues of a showdown that shared the stage of a pachyderm-pungent circus. "The only thing not ridiculous about the whole mess," he would say later, "was we won the game."

AFTERMATH

In its first 12 years, the NFL used the National Collegiate Athletic Association's rules. But temporary changes adopted for the 1932 NFL championship game were so successful that the league broke ranks with the NCAA and began reshaping the game and, coincidentally, saving the flagging league by making pro ball more exciting.

Many of the innovations that made the 1932 title game historic still stand. Others do not. Because the sideboards that enclosed the field could infringe on the action, teams were given the option of spotting a dead ball 15 yards in from the sideline. But it would cost them a down. Hash marks were here to stay—but it's hard to imagine a modern-day team huddling to weigh the pros and cons of foregoing a down for that privilege. (In 1933 the hash marks were set 10 yards from the sidelines; in '35 they were moved in another five yards; 10 years later, another five. Finally, in 1972, they were set at 70 feet, 9 inches from each sideline.) Because the makeshift field at Chicago Stadium was only 80 yards long, the uprights were placed on the goal lines rather than at the back of the end zone, a position change that resulted in twice as many field goals in 1933 as in 1932, and reduced the percentage of tie games in those years from 20% to less than 5%. In 1974 the NFL returned the posts to the back of the end zone in response to complaints that field goals dominated too many games. But the decision to allow Bronco Nagurski's pass from less than five yards behind the line of scrimmage went further than any other ad hoc rule change in modifying the way the game was played. In today's wide-open NFL, nearly twice as many yards are gained through the air as on the ground.

23 / 21
BEARS / GIANTS

To the college football poobahs who refused to open up their rules of play, the NFL offered an object lesson in the entertainment value of less tightly wrapped offenses: the championship game of 1933. After its first title matchup, a historic if not exactly rollicking 9–0 victory by the Chicago Bears over the Portsmouth Spartans in 1932, the NFL had liberalized the use of the forward pass. Now, when the top teams from the two new divisions clashed for the title at Wrigley Field, they had more options at their disposal. The result on this 19-degree, foggy Chicago day: six lead changes, one hook and numerous laterals, a flea-flicker and a center-eligible play before the outcome was decided on the final snap. Bears star Red Grange called it "the greatest game I've ever seen."

The visiting Giants had an offensive line that included four future Hall of Famers, and were led by rookie quarterback Harry Newman, an All-America from Michigan. Chicago was powered by the tackle-to-tackle bursts of fullback Bronko Nagurski. Once asked by teammates how he had become so strong, Nagurski told them he used to plow fields. His fellow Bears informed him that he wasn't the only player to have done that. Nagurski smiled and said, "Without a horse?"

Chicago used its field position to score two early field goals; the second, a 40-yarder by Jack Manders, was the longest of the season. The Giants took the lead back, 7–6, when Newman connected with Red Badgro on a 29-yard score. In the third quarter Manders, who had made only six field goals going into this game, drilled his third of the day. But back came the Giants to go up 14–9 after an eight-play, 61-yard drive.

Hewitt, one of the last NFL players to compete without a helmet, lateraled to Karr for the game-winning touchdown.

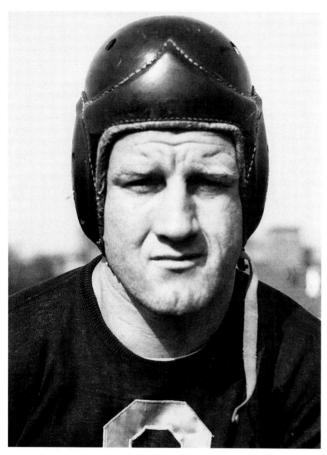
Nagurski claimed his strength came from a boyhood on the farm.

"That's when things became very strange," said Steve Owen, the New York right tackle and coach. Indeed, referee Tommy Hughitt almost got whiplash from constantly having to give each team covert clearance for its next rule-testing ploy.

Bears halfback George Corbett delivered the first jolting bolt, a 67-yard pass to Carl Brumbaugh. From the eight—and after getting the go-ahead from Hughitt—Nagurski charged the line, stopped, and fired a jump pass to rookie Bill Karr. The play that had been so controversial a year earlier was now strictly kosher, and it put the Bears up 16–14.

On its next series New York returned fire with what center Mel Hein called "the shortest forward pass on record." All six Giants linemen lined up to Hein's right, making him an eligible receiver. Standing like a T-formation quarterback, Newman took the snap and immediately slipped the ball back to Hein, who tucked it inside his jersey. Newman pretended to have fumbled, while 10 Bears swarmed the backfield to look for the ball. Hein

intended to stroll undetected to paydirt, but after a few yards he got excited and ran. "[Safety Keith] Molesworth saw me and knocked me down," Hein said. "I got about 30 yards, but didn't score."

More successful and far less scripted was the gambit New York used at the Bears' eight-yard line to go ahead 21–16 early in the fouth quarter. Newman handed off to halfback Ken Strong, the NFL's top scorer, who headed around left end. Hemmed in, he spied Newman open across the field and pitched the ball back to him, then streaked to the end zone. Newman, stunned, unloaded under pressure back to Strong, who made the grab and tumbled into the first-base dugout. "Newman to Strong to Newman to Strong," fumed Chicago coach George Halas. "Who would be foolish enough to dream up such a play?"

The Giants had ad-libbed the forerunner to the flea-flicker; now the Bears would sketch a blueprint for the hook-and-lateral. With less than three minutes to play and from the New York 34, Nagurski threw another jump pass, this time to Bill Hewitt, who saw that he was about to be tackled. He heaved a long lateral to Karr. Newman and Strong closed in to make the tackle, but Bears halfback Gene Ronzani, in Halas's words, "blocked Strong so hard that he crashed into the bleachers." The TD vaulted Chicago ahead 23–21.

The Giants liked that dodge so much that they tried to use it themselves to win the game. Newman, dangerous the whole game (12 of 17 for 201 yards), threw desperately to Dale Burnett over the middle at the Bears' 40. Grange, 30-years-old and a year away from retirement, saw Hein trailing and stayed one step ahead. While making the tackle Grange pinned Burnett's arms to stop him from lateraling. Halas proclaimed Red's Bear hug "the greatest defensive play I've ever seen."

The innovative end-to-end action prompted *The New York Times* to call the championship "a thrilling combat of forward passing skill, desperate line plunging and gridiron strategy that kept the chilled spectators on their feet in constant excitement." Or, as Hein put it, "It was kind of a screwy game all around."

Brumbaugh (8) was involved in several key plays for Chicago, including a 67-yard pass reception in the third quarter.

The New York Giants would compete in five of the NFL's first seven title games, including the first three. They won a rematch with Chicago in 1934, a game with an equally prominent—if slightly quirkier—place in NFL lore as the seesaw classic of the previous year. Known as the Sneaker Game, the '34 championship was held at the ice-covered Polo Grounds in nine-degree weather. His team having slipped and slid to a 10–3 deficit, New York coach Steve Owen had basketball shoes delivered to the Giants locker room at halftime. Their new-

AFTERMATH

found traction made the difference, and New York stormed back, scoring four fourth-quarter touchdowns to rout the Bears 30–13. The following year they met Detroit, whose gritty defense produced a 26–7 rout. When the Giants returned to the title game in 1938, a record 48,120 fans turned out. They were not disappointed, as New York defeated Green Bay in a thriller, 23–17. In a rematch the following year, Green Bay extracted revenge, 27–0. The Giants would go on to three title games in the '40s, all losses.

ONE-MAN GAMES

OVERVIEW

Football is at heart a team game, requiring the sort of intricate plotting and unity of purpose normally associated with soldiers on a mission, or ants at a picnic. But frequently a game becomes the stage on which the strutting and fretting of a single player emerges paramount. In some cases he will be remembered for sustained brilliance; in others, for a moment of inspiration that swung the outcome. And yet, among the thousands of individual performances that have stamped games, only a few stand out as truly transcendent.

Harold (Red) Grange didn't have to do much to make compelling theater of the Chicago Bears' 1925 date with the New York Giants. In fact, had he only donned a leather helmet and a navy-blue No. 77 jersey and high-stepped onto the Polo Grounds field for a snap or two, many of the 70,000 fans in attendance would have felt satisfied. The sheer magnitude of Grange's stardom was enough to pack the stands, and in the end sufficient to make the NFL a sporting staple in the nation's most populous and important city. Grange's performance—he had a 35-yard interception return for a TD while seeing limited action—was secondary to his mere presence.

Four decades later Bears coach George Halas had another prized rookie runner, but this time the hosannas came in the *wake* of the star's exploits. Twice before a player had scored six touchdowns in a single game, but neither of those prodigious scorers had the breathtaking flair of Gale Sayers, who glided supernaturally across a

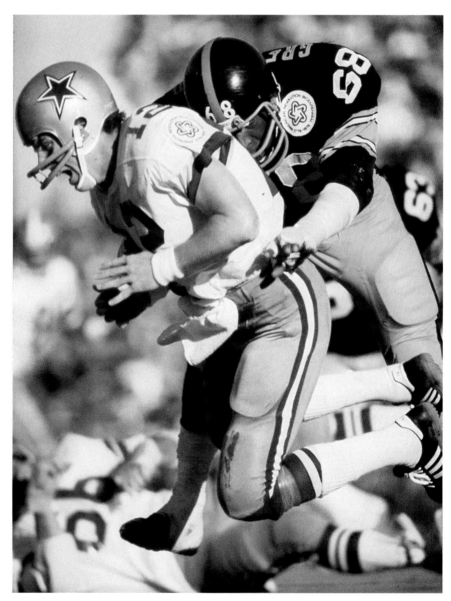

Swann's acrobatic grace (left) would not have led to victory were it not for defensive stalwarts such as L.C. Greenwood (above, tackling Roger Staubach).

Bradshaw (left) was brilliant in Super Bowl XIII, erasing all doubts about his intelligence under fire, but like many heroes, he needed some help, getting it from Dallas's Jackie Smith (above), whose dropped pass kept Pittsbugh in the lead.

muddy Wrigley Field, striking paydirt in every way imaginable against the San Francisco 49ers.

Likewise, style counted when Earl Campbell of the Houston Oilers bulled for 199 yards against Miami at the Astrodome in 1978. That total didn't come close to breaking the NFL's rushing record, but it did come in headline-grabbing fashion, on a Monday night, while the nation watched. With an electrifying 81-yard romp to seal Houston's victory, Campbell, a rookie, capped his coming-out party—and served notice to defenders that the league had a bruising new back who ran like a cross between Bronco Nagurski and Jim Brown.

A pair of Steelers used the grandest stage of all to show their mettle: a Super Bowl against the Cowboys. Questions about wide receiver Lynn Swann's forti-

tude were erased by his four catches, three of them spectacular, in Pittsburgh's 21–17 victory in Super Bowl X at Miami. At the Orange Bowl three years later, quarterback Terry Bradshaw responded to sniping about his intelligence by surgically dissecting the Dallas secondary in the Steelers' 35–31 win.

George Blanda's contributions to the Oakland Raiders' 23–20 defeat of Cleveland in 1970 weren't so extensive. He came in to play quarterback in the fourth quarter, and though he threw a TD pass, he also tossed an interception. On the last play from scrimmage, however, Blanda made the game his, kicking the winning field goal from 52 yards out. Oh, and there's this: He was 43 years old.

Which proves that heroes, like their heroics, come in more than one form.

10 / 7
BEARS / GIANTS

They came from St. Louis, Cleveland, Cincinnati and Detroit. From Pittsburgh, Baltimore, Washington and Buffalo. From Boston, Providence, Syracuse and Hartford. More than 100 reporters flocked to New York's Polo Grounds to bear witness to a sporting event that had previously drawn little interest: a professional football game. "Newspapers would throw our stories in the wastebasket when we'd send them over game information," Bears coach George Halas said years later. "The college game was what everyone cared about."

The public, however, was about to reverse its opinion of the NFL. Only 14 days earlier, C.C. (Cash and Carry) Pyle, a movie theater owner who sported spats on his feet and a diamond stickpin in his lapel, had persuaded a certain Illinois senior running back to matriculate to the pros. (Until then teams drew their players from colleges in the teams' immediate vicinity and from so-called "sandlotters," pro and semi-pro players who were willing to risk life and limb for laughably low sums of money.) The Illini coach, Bob Zuppke, argued against making such a move. "Football," he told his charge, "isn't meant to be played for money." But Pyle had offered up a roseate vision tinged with green—a coast-to-coast tour featuring 19 games, with guaranteed fees and percentages of the gate that would yield more than $100,000 for 61 days' work. For four years, Pyle had given Harold (Red) Grange free passes to the movies; now he would parlay everybody's All-America into his meal ticket.

There could be no better image upgrade for the struggling six-year-old league than the Galloping Ghost, he of the swiveling hips and elusive stride, the master of the "limp leg," the trick of offering a gam to a would-be tackler, then pulling it as away soon as the tackler commited to a direction. The modest son of a Wheaton, Ill., police chief, Grange was a

Grange was a genuine triple threat as rusher, kick returner and passer (right).

48

triple threat whose exploits with the Illini had become the nation's fixation. "Perhaps Babe Ruth is better known," wrote *The New York Times*, "but even that is questionable."

On Nov. 21, the 22-year-old Grange played his last game for the Illini, rushing for 192 yards against Ohio State and intercepting a pass in the end zone to preserve a 14–9 victory at Columbus. He joined the Bears in Chicago the following week, on Thanksgiving day, attracting a standing-room-only crowd of 36,000—the highest turnout in pro football history—for a tilt with the crosstown Cardinals.

Pyle's barnstorming brainstorm boomed. The Red Rover drew another 28,000 spectators for an exhibition game at Cubs Park, racked up four touchdowns against a mortician's all-star team in St. Louis and scored both TDs in a win at Philadelphia, where 35,000 showed up despite a vicious rainstorm. From those four dates Grange earned $52,000.

All of that was but a warmup, though, for the Ghost's appearance at the Polo Grounds. Colorful bunting floated from the field boxes

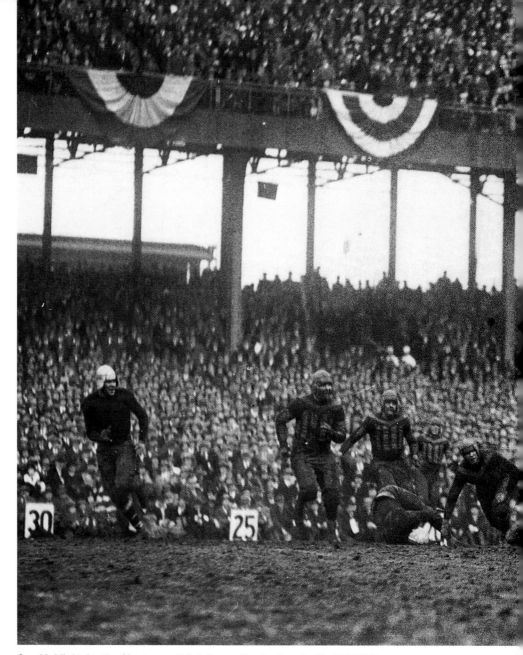

One highlight for the Giants was this interception by New York's Phil White.

and pennants waved from the goal posts as the crowd began pouring in three hours before kickoff. And in. And in. The stadium's seating capacity of 65,000 was reached after the game started, and some 8,000 seat-less souls wedged in as well, setting yet another pro football attendance record (and leaving Grange $30,000 richer). Bankers and bakers, socialites and newsboys, diehard fans and pigskin neophytes all craned for a glimpse of the glamorous Grange, "the youth who had risen from the obscurity of a Middle Western village to the position of the most advertised athlete the world probably has ever known," according to the *Times*.

Grange's performance was equal parts ghost and gallop. Already worn out from the tour, he played only the first

quarter and parts of two others in Chicago's 19–7 victory. Still, No. 77 accounted for 128 yards on rushes, runbacks, passes, receptions and a 35-yard interception that he returned for a touchdown.

His traveling act went on, packing the stands and converting the curious. But Grange's ability to make New Yorkers take notice of the NFL may have saved the league's most crucial franchise. Until the Rover romped on that muddy field, the largest turnout for a Giants home date had been 28,000. "Football would have caught on," Wellington Mara, the son of the Giants' owner, Tim, said. "But I don't know when, and I don't know how. This surely accelerated how quickly pro football became a national sport and a popular sport."

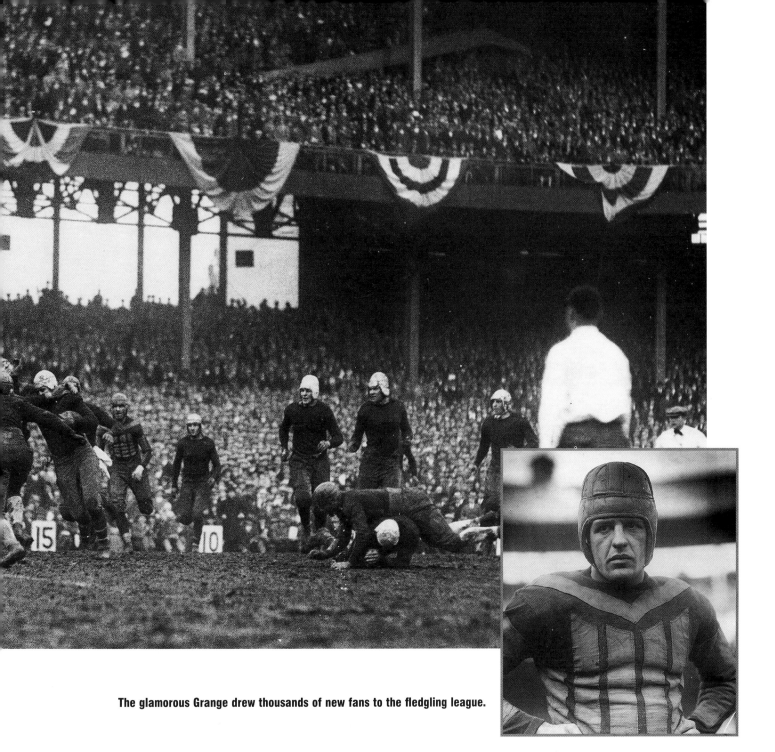

The glamorous Grange drew thousands of new fans to the fledgling league.

During "the 66 days that made pro football"—as *Sports Illustrated* later called Grange's first pro stint—more than 400,000 fans paid to cheer the former Illini half-back as he administered CPR to the young but moribund NFL. By the end of the grueling 19-game barnstorming tour, Grange's agent, C.C. Pyle, was sanguine enough about the professional game's prospects that he created a rival league, the AFL, and set the Galloping Ghost up as the marquee player for the

AFTERMATH

New York Yankees in 1926. The team had moderate success, but the league floundered. By the next season, Grange was back in the NFL, where he would suffer a crippling knee injury against his former team, the Bears. After a year-long hiatus, Grange took George Halas up on an invitation to play again for Chicago. Although he was no longer a standout, he did help the Bears win titles by catching the winning pass in the 1932 title game and making a game-saving tackle to end the '33 championship game.

Only twice in the NFL's 46 seasons had a player scored six touchdowns in one game. Now, in the slop of rain-soaked Wrigley Field, a rookie running back for the hometown Bears was aching to score his seventh TD of the day. Chicago had the ball on San Francisco's three-yard line with 1:56 remaining. The 49ers trailed 54–20, and their defense was worn down from three hours of sloshing around in futile pursuit of six feet and 200 pounds of pure sorcery. The drenched crowd of 43,400 clamored for George (Papa Bear) Halas to put Gale Sayers back in for one more play.

A few weeks before the 1965 NFL draft Halas, Chicago's owner and coach, hadn't decided whom to choose with the team's pair of first-round picks. The No. 3 choice would almost certainly be Dick Butkus, the ferocious middle linebacker from Illinois. Halas wanted to use No. 4 on Sayers, the son of an Omaha mechanic and a housewife, who had just led Kansas to the Big Eight title. Halas simply wasn't sure the kid was for real. "We thought perhaps some of his performance was just luck," Halas said. "Then I saw a highlight film on him where he made two moves in one stride and ran 95 yards, and that was it."

At Chicago's training camp Sayers proved that seeing was believing. He was durable and quietly determined and, said Halas, "He'll block any s.o.b. who's in front of him." Above all Papa Bear got big eyes from watching the 45-degree cuts Sayers could make without losing speed, leaving tacklers to guess which direction he might choose next. Draw a bead on Sayers's hip and you might snatch air; lunge for his thigh and you could wind up with handfuls of turf. His opponents soon had a nickname for him. They called him Magic.

In Sayers's first exhibition game for Chicago, he

Sayers went airborne for touchdown No. 5, a one-yard plunge that left him one short of the NFL mark.

52

All around the league, crowds were excited by his exploits. In a packed Yankee Stadium on Nov. 28, Sayers rushed for 113 yards and two touchdowns, outproducing Giants halfback Tucker Frederickson, the 1965 draft's top pick. "I can't define my running style," Sayers said in an expansive moment. "Really, I don't know where I'm going. I go where my feet take me. I like to think if my blockers can give me 18 inches of clearance, I've got a shot to break a long one."

A fortnight later the Niners came to town. Sayers hadn't started during San Francisco's 52–24 rout earlier in the season. Now revenge would be messy. Chicago's equipment manager handed out shoes with extra-long nylon cleats to

Just when Sayers seemed trapped...

Sayers's six-touchdown performance forced even the hard-bitten Halas to resort to superlatives.

returned a kickoff 93 yards for a touchdown, brought a punt back 77 yards and tossed a 25-yard TD pass on an option play. Still, the 70-year-old Halas stuck to his guns and brought him along slowly. Sayers didn't make his first start until the third game of the season, when he scored both of the Bears' touchdowns in a loss to the Packers. A week later he raced 80 yards with a screen pass and threw for another TD. The following Sunday he scored four times against the Vikings. "How about that, Gale?" a TV reporter asked afterward. "Wasn't that 96-yard run about your biggest thrill ever?"

"No," Sayers said, "I've had lots of thrills."

facilitate cutting in the slop. Even in good conditions Sayers ran flat-footed. Today he would have to dig in his heels still more.

In the first quarter Sayers gathered in a screen pass from Rudy Bukich in the right flat, made a diagonal cut left past linebacker Matt Hazeltine and churned up 80 yards of mud in the Niners' faces. "He looks no different from any other runner when he's coming at you," said defensive back George Donnelly. "But when he gets there, he's not there. He's gone." By the end of the third quarter Sayers had racked up four more touchdowns: a 21-yard burst off left tackle, a seven-yard blast past Hazeltine, a 50-yard sprint and a one-yard plunge. "I can still see the 49ers sloshing around," he said. "It seemed like everyone was slipping but me."

Sayers saved something special for TD No. 6. He fielded a punt in the rain at his own 15, ran right, shook off a 49ers tackler, headed straight down that side of the field and then proved that he was indeed supernatural by traversing the sodden pitch at midfield and making his way down the left sideline to score. "I've always been proud that I had enough left in the fourth quarter to run that one in," Sayers said.

He had struck paydirt by receiving, running and returning. Though he had touched the ball only 16 times he had amassed 336 yards: 113 on nine rushes, 89 on two catches,

134 on five punt returns. In his eleventh NFL start he had matched the record single-game TD total shared by Chicago Cardinals fullback Ernie Nevers (1929) and Cleveland Browns running back Dub Jones (1951).

But there would be no record-breaking TD No. 7. Halas, who had doubted this rookie before the draft, now realized he was too valuable to risk running him again against a proud, mud-caked defense. Halas had seen too many things happen in his nearly 50 years of pro football— though nothing like Sayers slicing through the 49ers that day. "It isn't often that the Bears break a tradition," he said, "but this was the greatest football exhibition I have ever seen by one man in one game."

he would shift direction...

leaving defenders off balance...

and Sayers on his way to the end zone.

Pro scouts doubted whether Gale Sayers could make the jump from the University of Kansas to the NFL because they weren't sure Sayers, a brilliant finesse runner, could withstand the physical pounding running backs invariably suffered in the NFL. What they failed to consider was that defenders hit the air around Sayers more often than they connected with the man himself. Possessed with blinding speed, a kind of liquid agility that allowed him to change direction in overdrive, and good hands, Sayers was a Hall-of-Fame triple threat. For

AFTERMATH

many ground-game aficionados he is the greatest back of all time. He certainly was one of the most entertaining to watch, with his trademark twisting, turning, now-you-see-me-now-you-don't gallops to the end zone that left a trail of fallen defenders in his wake. Sadly, Sayers suffered a severe knee injury in 1968. He recovered to rush for more than 1,000 yards in a dismal 1969 season for the 1–13 Bears, but another knee injury, in 1970, spelled the end of his great career. He retired in 1971 after just seven NFL seasons.

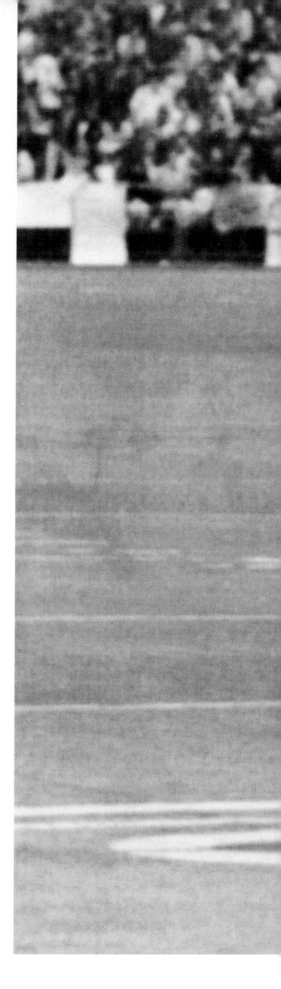

OILERS / DOLPHINS

There was no mystery about what Houston coach Bum Phillips would do. His team was stuck deep in its own territory, clinging to a 28–23 lead over Miami with less than two minutes to go and in desperate need of a few clock-consuming first downs. Phillips played his football like a riverboat gambler with his cards showing, and Bum's ace was there for 42 million people sitting in their living rooms on Monday night to see. "I don't know if Earl Campbell is in a class by himself," Phillips said, "but it sure don't take long to call the roll."

There was no mystery about Campbell either. What you saw was what you got: a 5' 11", 225-pound raging bull of a rookie tailback, Texas born and bred, so plain-spoken his nickname was Easy Earl. He had no use, or need, for subtlety when he touched the ball, and for the sake of piling up yardage, coaches like Phillips would put it in his hands 30 or more times a game. The Oilers had drafted Campbell, the 1977 Heisman Trophy winner at Texas, after dealing four draft choices and starting tight end Jimmie Giles to Tampa Bay for the rights to the No. 1 choice.

To celebrate the arrival of Howard Cosell, Frank Gifford, Don Meredith and the Monday night audience, 50,290 rabid Oiler fans choked the Astrodome with pale blue pompons and filled it with Luv-Ya-Blue shrieks louder than a cattle stampede.

Both teams were fighting to make the playoffs—Miami was 8–3, Houston 7–4—but Campbell was the drawing card. He had, in the words of Cosell, "taken the league by storm." With 945 yards he was already within 217 of the rookie rushing record set by San Diego's Don Woods in 1974. Houston center Carl Mauck had blocked for both backs. "Don was like a

The sight of Campbell gathering a head of steam was surely one of the NFL's most fearsome.

Cadillac," Mauck said. "But Earl is like a Sherman tank."

Indeed, what made Campbell so riveting to watch wasn't just the yardage he could pile up, but also the punishment he could inflict while doing it. Rams linebacker Isiah Robertson had already branded him "the toughest guy to tackle in the NFL," after Campbell leveled him on one fourth-down run. "I was right where I was supposed to be," Robertson said. "I came up and boom, boom, boom, he buried me."

The sixth of 11 children raised in Tyler by a God-fearing single mom in a shack situated between a peach orchard and a salvage yard, Campbell led John Tyler High to the state's 4A title as a senior. With the Long-

horns he roared to a school record 4,444 yards, and in the pros he showed no sign of being slowed. Campbell's Lone Star state roots made him all the more beloved in Houston, where he endorsed everything from ice cream to snuff. NO. 34—A GUSHER OF A RUSHER, read one sign at the Astrodome.

For the sake of drama, the Dolphins were kind enough to provide Campbell with a foil: 11-year veteran quarterback Bob Griese, who would complete 23 of 33 passes for 349 yards and two touchdowns. For three quarters the teams swapped TDs, scoring one apiece in each period. Campbell had a pair of scores on short runs. With 12:25 to play in the fourth, Dolphins linebacker A.J. Duhe sacked

With Campbell piling up the yards on the ground, Pastorini had to take to the air only 16 times.

Dan Pastorini in the end zone for a safety to make it 23–21. Campbell had failed to make the block, and he stewed about his mistake. But Phillips wasn't fazed. "That safety wasn't gonna decide the game, I knew that for sure," he said afterward. "Earl was gonna decide it."

Campbell was getting stronger as the game wore on. He had 44 yards at halftime, 74 by the end of the third period. When the Oilers got the ball back on their own 20 with 11:06 to play, Campbell ground out 36 of the 80 yards on an 11-play drive, including the final 12 off right tackle. That put Houston up 28–23. Griese marched Miami right back, but with 3:05 left he was picked off by linebacker Steve Kiner at the Houston seven. Three first downs would chew up the rest of the game.

Phillips's scheme was not long on nuance. There were no hidden ball tricks or misdirection plays or flea flickers. Pastorini had thrown just 16 passes; 27 times he had handed off or quick-pitched to Campbell. Facing second-and-9 with 1:22 remaining, Pastorini called "Pitch 28." Campbell rumbled toward right tackle for his 10th carry in the team's last 14 snaps. He was looking for a few tough yards.

The hole opened and Campbell drove through it. Cornerback Norris Thomas tried to stop him, for naught; so did defensive back Curtis Johnson. Linebacker Steve Towle flailed at Campbell as well. An unmatched package of power and speed fighting through exhaustion, Campbell pounded 81 yards down the sideline into the end zone. The Oiler trainers had to help him back to the bench.

He finished with 199 yards rushing and four touchdowns

Campbell's 199 rushing yards was among the most impressive Monday Night performances in the history of that showcase.

on 28 carries, earning a win for the Oilers and raves from Cosell, Gifford and Meredith. "That game changed my career," Campbell said. "When those announcers put me on that elite level, then I started to feel comfortable. I knew I could never be lower than that—and worked at it to stay up there."

The Tyler Rose would go on to break the rookie rushing record in 1978, finishing with 1,450 yards in 15 games and leading the Oilers to the AFC championship game. He also won the league MVP award that year and made the Pro Bowl, an honor he would receive in five of his first six seasons. When football fans discuss the greatest backs of all time, Campbell and his tree-trunk thighs invariably enter the conversation. Perhaps the single strike against Campbell is that he thrilled us for only eight seasons. Being the "toughest guy to tackle in the NFL" carried a price, and even though he missed just six of 115 games in his career because of injuries, his characteristic bruising style eventually caught up with him. Campbell called it quits in 1985, but not before guaranteeing himself a bust in Canton, Ohio (he was inducted into the Hall of Fame in 1991). The league's leading rusher in each of his first three seasons, Campbell gained 1,934 yards in 1980, still the third-best single-season total of all time. His career total of 9,407 rushing yards puts him at No. 13 on the alltime career list.

AFTERMATH

STEELERS / COWBOYS

35 / 31

After guiding Pittsburgh to victories in Super Bowls IX and X and as many wins as any quarterback in history, 30-year-old Terry Bradshaw might have thought he had dispelled any doubts about his football acumen. He hadn't. True, no one called him a dumb blond anymore, but that was only because he had lost most of his hair. Here, just days before Supe XIII at the Orange Bowl in Miami, Dallas linebacker Thomas (Hollywood) Henderson was trashing Bradshaw's intelligence at the most basic level. "He couldn't spell 'cat,'" Henderson said, "if you spotted him the 'c' and the 'a.'"

Henderson's head shot was the most widely circulated quote of the fourteen-day media feeding frenzy. Bradshaw tried vainly to shrug it off. "Sure it hurts to be called dumb," he said. "But the only way to get rid of a reputation is show everybody they're wrong."

There can be no greater crucible in the nation for forming—or revising—a reputation in sports than the Super Bowl, and there was no greater Super Bowl for doing just that than XIII, a thriller that featured not only the decade's glamor teams but also the year's powerhouses. Pittsburgh had gone 14–2 in the regular season and blitzed through two playoff games by an aggregate score of 67–15; the Flex defense of defending champ Dallas had just helped the Cowboys throttle the Rams 28–0 in the NFC title game. The much-anticipated Super Bowl clash drew 74% of TV viewers at the time of the game, a figure that hasn't been surpassed.

Henderson, a fourth-year speedbacker from tiny Langston (Okla.) University, sensed the image-making moment, grabbing headlines with blowtorch subtlety. He called Steelers All-Pro linebacker Jack Lambert "a toothless chimpanzee," and said reserve tight end Randy Gross-

Bradshaw ended all doubts about his abilities, throwing for 318 yards and a gaudy four touchdowns.

60

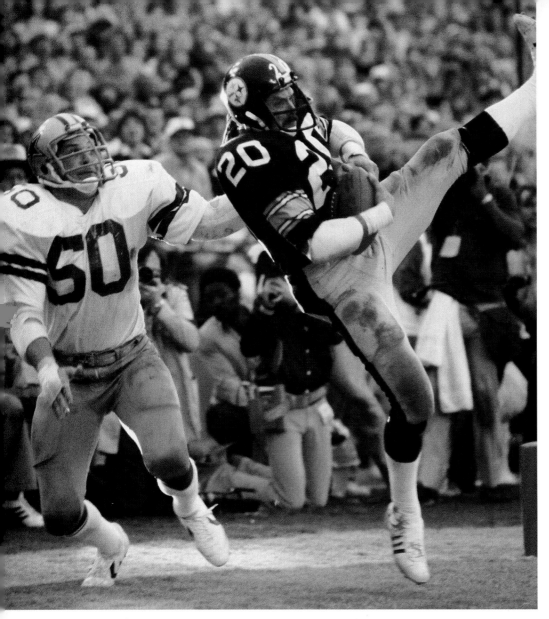

Bleier's touchdown catch put the Steelers ahead 21–14 at halftime.

First came an interception and then a fumble, which the Cowboys converted for a touchdown that was the first score allowed all season by the Steelers in the first quarter. On the next series Henderson, swooping in, stripped the ball from Bradshaw again; linebacker Mike Hegman plucked it out of the air and ran 37 yards to the end zone to make it 14–7. Bradshaw, his left shoulder hurt on the play, seemed to be losing his grip.

No one had ever doubted Bradshaw's prodigious talent. He was the first pick in the draft out of Louisiana Tech in 1970, and he was big, mobile, rifle-armed and tough. The Flex sacked him four times, but he refused to back off, rallying to pass for a pair of TDs before halftime that put Pittsburgh on top, 21–14. "I've never ever thrown well against the Cowboys," Bradshaw said after the game. "I've always tried not to lose to them. This year I learned you can't play well if you don't relax and let your abilities play for you."

man "only plays when someone dies or breaks his leg."

Henderson's antithesis was the Cowboys' backup tight end, Jackie Smith. A 38-year-old pro's pro, Smith was a Hall of Fame candidate with 16 seasons and 480 catches for the St. Louis Cardinals to his credit. Only four months before, he had been selling real estate and running a restaurant in St. Louis. But Dallas coach Tom Landry had coaxed Smith out of retirement with the prospect of his playing in just this sort of game, where rings were won and reputations forever altered.

The south Florida skies cleared before kickoff, and Bradshaw came out flinging. He floated a 28-yard beauty to John Stallworth in the first quarter to put Pittsburgh up 7–0. But he followed that with three straight turnovers that seemed to affirm Henderson's abecedarian doubts.

Dallas came back, charging to the Pittsburgh 10-yard line with 2:46 to play in the third quarter. On third down Smith slipped into the end zone uncovered, as unnoticed by the Steel Curtain secondary as he had been by the press for two weeks. Roger Staubach's pass was soft and low and catchable. Smith slipped slightly and the ball struck his hip pads, then his chest. On his knees, Smith dropped it. Instead of six points, the Cowboys settled for a field goal.

That wasn't the Cowboys' only costly second-half flub. Bradshaw guided the Steelers on a 61-yard drive in the fourth quarter, aided by a controversial interference call against cornerback Benny Barnes. On the ensuing kickoff defensive tackle Randy White, stationed in the middle of the return team despite sporting a cast on his broken left

Tony Hill highstepped his way around the Pittsburgh defense and into the end zone to tie the game at 7–all in the first quarter.

hand, mishandled Roy Gerela's soft line drive. The Steelers recovered at the Dallas 18.

Bradshaw immediately hit receiver Lynn Swann, and in 19 seconds Pittsburgh had scored two TDs to lead 35–17. "The thing about Bradshaw that day," Landry would say, "was his accuracy downfield and his ability to make big plays."

Staubach passed for two touchdowns of his own in the next 6:29, but Pittsburgh running back Rocky Bleier

recovered an onside kick with 22 seconds to play that sealed the victory. The 66 points scored were twice the average of the previous 12 Super Bowls, and the 674 yards of offense were unprecedented. Bradshaw, the game's MVP, set records with four TD tosses and 318 yards passing. Vindication was complete, and sweet. "Ask Thomas Henderson," Bradshaw said as the final seconds ticked off the clock, "if I can spell now."

Besides Bradshaw's arm and his superb receivers ... the other thing that helped defeat the Cowboys was the touchdown they blew late in the third quarter, which would have tied the score 21–21. Smith, the marvelous old former St. Louis Cardinal whom Dallas had called out of retirement in September, flat-out dropped Staubach's pass in the end zone.

The play came from Landry, and it was an inspired call. The ball was on

In SI's Words

the Pittsburgh 10, third and three. Landry sent in an extra tight end, Smith, indicating a run. Dallas lined up with Scott Laidlaw as a single set-back and Dorsett went in motion to his right. But instead of handing off to Laidlaw or passing in the flat to Dorsett, the most likely eventualities, Staubach threw over the middle to the 38-year-old Smith who was wide open.

However, the ball was low and slightly behind Smith. Staubach says he threw it too softly, and that's why Smith, who was on his knees, dropped it.

"He was so open I could have punted it to him," said Staubach sorrowfully.

Smith could only say, "It was a beautiful play that Coach Landry conceived. When I slipped, I guess I was just trying to be overcautious, and that's why I dropped it."

—Dan Jenkins
January 29, 1979

Shortly before the start of the 1970 season, Oakland managing general partner Al Davis called George Blanda in to tell him that he'd been placed on waivers. Davis explained that the move had been strictly a matter of procedure, that he had no intention of really letting his placekicker and No. 2 quarterback go. "This is the worst thing that's ever happened to me!" Blanda screamed, incensed not so much at what Davis had done, but at what the other 25 teams in the league hadn't: None had bothered to claim him.

Blanda had been dumped by teams twice before. When Chicago released him in 1959, he sat out a year until a new league began play. "The AFL's caliber must be low," Bears coach George Halas said. "Even Blanda can make a team." Eight years later he was waived by the Oilers, whom he had led to the championship in '61. "Blanda refuses to grow old gracefully," muttered a Houston coach. The Raiders had picked him up for a "unnamed player," but now Davis too was fiddling with his walking papers. And to top it off, Blanda's birthday was only one week away. He would be turning 43.

"You've made it very clear to me that you see me as an ancient quarterback on his last legs, and *I'm not*," Blanda shouted at Davis. "But maybe it's too much trouble to convince you." Hell, he would quit first; after all his wife, Betty, had been after him to retire for, um, 11 years. Davis assured him that he was a vital part of the team and urged him to reconsider. A day later, Blanda had cooled down, changed his mind and, for the 21st time, was gearing up for a season of pro football.

George Blanda's longevity wasn't the result of clean living: He smoked a pack or two a day and had sipped bourbon since his college days at Kentucky. It had to do with his upbringing in Youngwood, Pa., where Blanda was

Blanda's 42-yard field goal in the second quarter was one of two he kicked before the 52-yard game-winner.

toughened up by six brothers and taught the value of hard work by his father, a coal miner. The years (and years, and years) had in no way diminished his love for competition and how he made a living. "Sure, pro football is violent," Blanda said. "That's one of the nicest things about it."

In the Raiders' second game Blanda failed to convert with a last-minute, 32-yard field goal try. "He appears unsteady at field goal time, like Ben Hogan hanging over a putt," one critic wrote. Then with Oakland and Pittsburgh tied 7–all in Game 6, Daryle Lamonica went down, and Blanda relieved him at quarterback. He threw a pair of TD passes and the Raiders roared to a 31–14 win. One week later, the Raiders trailed arch-rival Kansas City 17–14 with three seconds to play. Blanda drilled a 48-yard field goal to salvage a tie.

Two Sundays, two dramatic blows for a generation. The Over-40 Fan Club from Los Angeles wired Blanda: ON

Wells caught a 14-yard pass from Blanda to tie the score with 1:19 remaining and set up the dramatic finish.

AFTERMATH

Heartening oldsters from coast-to-coast, 43-year-old George Blanda enjoyed a magical run in the middle of the 1970 season, saving five straight games with his last-minute heroics. Oakland's dramatic victory over Cleveland was the third stop on the Blanda Revival Tour. The following week against Denver, he came off the bench in the final minute, his team trailing 19–17, and threw a touchdown pass to Fred Biletnikoff to beat the Broncos 24–19. In Oakland the week after that, Blanda calmly punched a 19-yard field goal through the uprights as time expired, giving Oakland a 20–17 win. He closed out the year as the oldest quarterback ever to appear in an NFL title game, accounting for all of the Raiders' points in a 27–17 loss to Baltimore in the AFC championship game. Not suprisingly, Blanda was named 1970 NFL Player of the Year. Having entered pro football in 1949 with the likes of Y.A. Tittle and Bobby Layne, Blanda left it in 1976, just one week shy of his 49th birthday, with players such as Ken (The Snake) Stabler and Terry Bradshaw calling the signals.

BEHALF OF ALL THE OTHER SENILE OLD WRECKS, WE SALUTE YOU! When Cleveland arrived at Oakland-Alameda County Coliseum the next Sunday, a banner flapped in the breeze: WELCOME TO THE OLD FOLKS HOME.

Blanda loathed the Browns, who had once separated his shoulder, inflicting the only serious injury of his career. The guys back at the Youngwood VFW measured players by their performances against Pittsburgh and Cleveland, and Blanda had already disposed of the Steelers this season. But he had never beaten the Browns. With Oakland down 17–13, Lamonica was badly blind-sided and coach John Madden was once again hollering for his quadregenarian quarterback. But Blanda failed to move the Raiders, the Browns kicked a field goal to go up 20–13 and, on his next series, Blanda threw an interception.

With four minutes remaining, the Raiders regained possession. Eschewing the run, Blanda quickly marched Oakland 50 yards to the Browns' 31. On fourth-and-16 he delivered an awkward, off-balance lob to Fred Biletnikoff for 17 yards. Madden called Blanda over to the sidelines where he sagged to his knees in exhaustion. Blanda told Madden that he was would call for the same

The flesh needed oxygen, but the spirit was very willing, as Blanda took a breather.

pass pattern—99 in Y—until the Raiders reached the end zone. One play later they were in. Wide receiver Warren Wells caught Blanda's low bullet in the end zone, and with 1:19 to play the game was tied at 20–all.

The Browns' Bill Nelsen then made a disastrous throw and cornerback Kent McCloughan picked it off. With the ball on the Cleveland 49 and less than 16 seconds remaining, Blanda, out of timeouts, completed a four-yarder to running back Hewritt Dixon, but there was an illegal procedure penalty on the play. Cleveland coach Blanton Collier could refuse the flag and let Blanda try a 56-yard field goal to win the game. Or he could take the penalty, pushing Blanda's attempt back

to 61 yards but also giving Oakland one more play. "I couldn't believe it when they took the penalty," Madden said.

On the next snap Blanda threw nine yards to Dixon, who raced out of bounds to stop the clock. Blanda lined up for a 52-yard field goal, the longest attempt of his four years with the Raiders. With three seconds left, his 43-year-old right foot sent the ball sailing toward the uprights. In the Oakland radio booth, Bill King made the call. "That's got a chance. That is—GOOD!" he said. "Holy Toledo! The place has gone wild! Whee-e-e! I don't believe it!… The Oakland Raiders 23, the Cleveland Browns 20. George Blanda has just been elected KING OF THE WORLD!"

STEELERS / COWBOYS

21 / 17

January 18, 1976

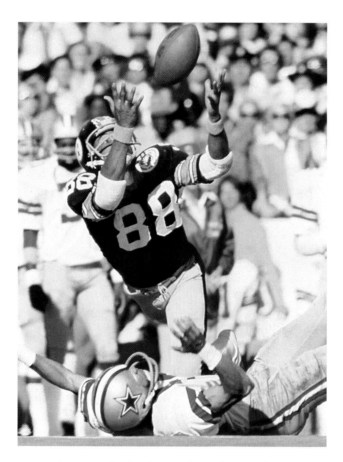

In 1975, Oakland Raiders defensive back George Atkinson had knocked Swann cold with a vicious head tackle, prompting Pittsburgh coach Chuck Noll to decry the "criminal element" in football. (Atkinson filed suit against Noll for slander.) This was his second concussion and Swann, only 25 and two years out of USC, briefly contemplated retirement. Instead, he spoke out against the "intentional acts of violence." Some defenders around the league figured his skull was as thin as his skin and marked him as fair game, a "paperhead."

Any doubts about the 5' 11", 180-pound Swann's toughness would have come as a surprise to the Steelers. "The licks Lynn takes, sometimes he looks like a baton being twirled out there," said guard Sam Davis. But days before Super Bowl X in Miami, Swann's world was still spinning from yet another concussion courtesy of a Raider assault in the AFC championship game, and it was unclear whether he would suit up.

During the Super Bowl buildup, Dallas safety Cliff Harris tried to further penetrate Swann's head. "Getting hit really hard has to be in the back of his mind," he said. Those words only riled

His mother wanted a daughter and gave him a girl's name. He wore a gold pendant inscribed with his own poetry. And he tap-danced, sipped champagne and slipped into white-tie-and-tails at the drop of a hat. Other players had performed elegantly on the field and relished the finer things in life off it, and little was made of their cultivated pursuits. But Pittsburgh wide receiver Lynn Curtis Swann had further distinguished himself as a target among the league's hard guys. He had become known as a player who couldn't take a hit.

Aerial artistry: Swann soared over Mark Washington (right) before making the tumbling catch (above) for 53 yards.

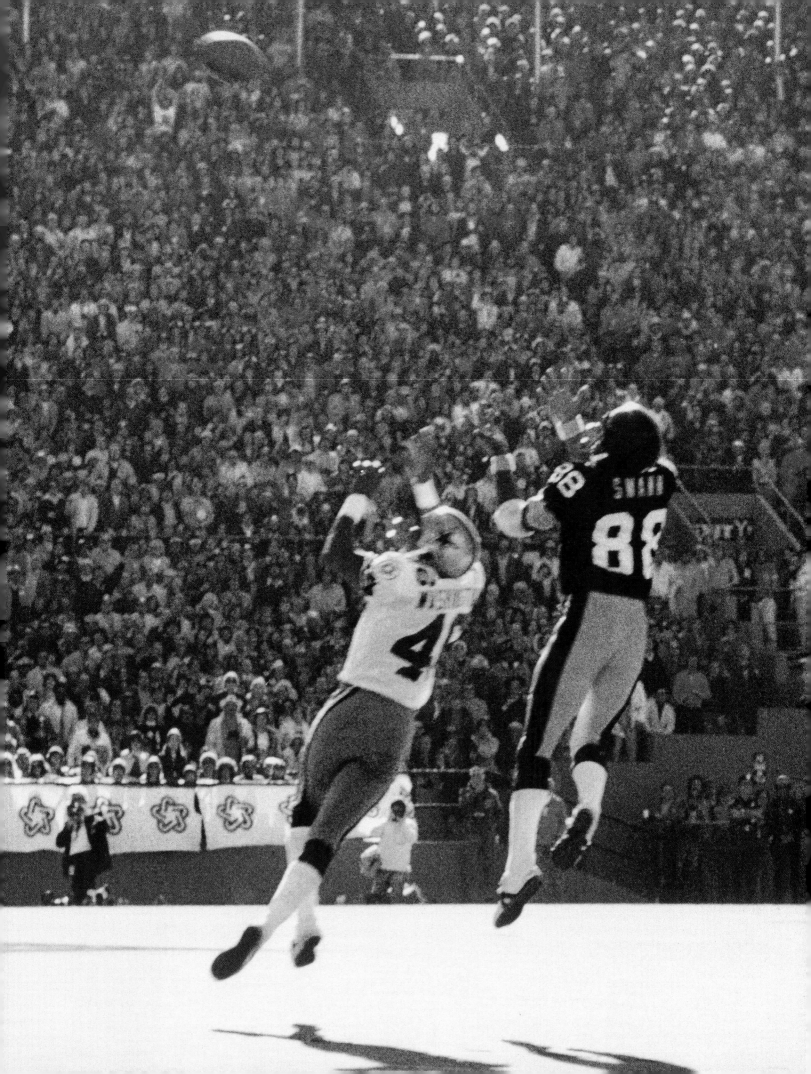

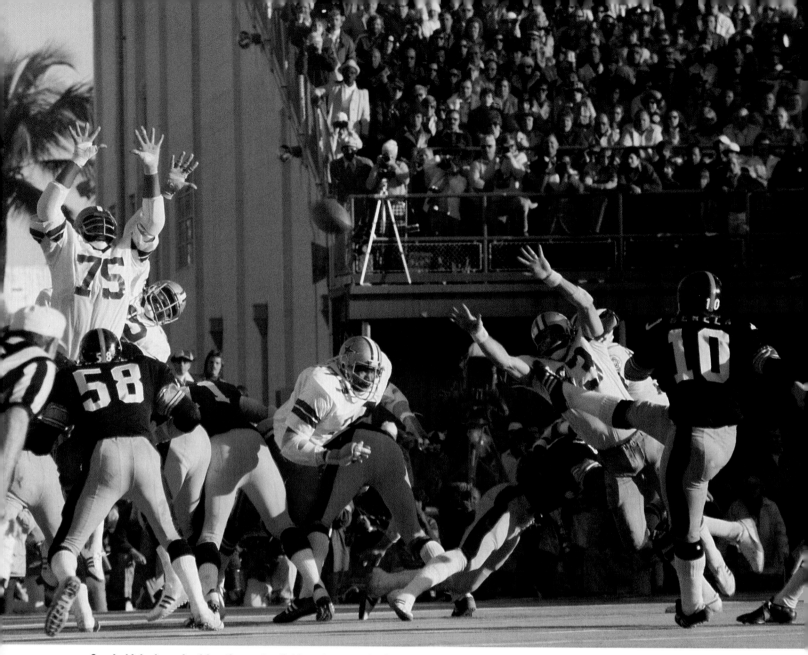

Gerela kicked a pair of fourth-quarter field goals to put the Steelers in the lead for good.

Swann, who made his living where few paperheads dared tread: over the middle. Two hours before the kickoff at the Orange Bowl, he took a nap in the locker room. He woke feeling refreshed and sharp and ready to shred a Cowboy defense bent on making him feel perishable.

The film *Black Sunday* used Super Bowl X as its backdrop, and a dark mood did pervade the game. Dallas coach Tom Landry had revamped his team with a crew of ornery rookies known as The Dirty Dozen and a new-fangled shotgun attack. Landry's gimmickry only offended the Steel Curtain's saturnine middle linebacker, Jack Lambert. "They mess up your head too much," he said. "If they beat you, you feel like you've been tricked instead of whipped. I hate teams like that."

While tempers rose and fists flew the whole sunshiny day, the refs dropped just two flags (both against Dallas) and play was remarkably crisp. The Cowboys scored first on a 29-yard pass from Roger Staubach to Drew Pearson. While Pittsburgh's offense misfired, the Dallas D zeroed in. After one early route, Harris snarled at Swann, "You're lucky you didn't come back on that ball because I'm gonna take a shot at you. You better watch your head."

As a high school student in San Mateo, Calif., Swann had won the state long jump championship and, at only 5'10", could dunk a basketball. He also studied ballet and gymnastics, which had enhanced his body control. Facing a third down, Pittsburgh quarterback Terry Bradshaw threw a deep sideline pass to Swann, who was covered tightly by cornerback Mark Washington. With his momentum carrying him out of play, Swann soared above Washington, twisted in midair, snagged the ball and then dragged both feet in bounds. Many consider it the greatest Super Bowl catch ever made.

Three plays later Bradshaw tossed seven yards to tight end Randy Grossman, and the game was tied. In the second quarter, Swann made another highlight grab, a tumbling, juggling 53-yarder, but Pittsburgh couldn't convert it into points and trailed 10–7 at halftime. The Steelers were up 15–10 after Reggie Harrison blocked a punt for a safety, and Roy Gerela nailed a pair of field goals.

With just over three minutes left in the game, the Steelers were on their own 36, facing third-and-four. The percentages said go for something short and safe to gain a fresh set of downs. So Bradshaw called 69 Maximum Flanker Post: a bomb to Swann. Dallas red-dogged, with linebacker D.D. Lewis charging from Bradshaw's blind side, and Harris on his heels. Sensing Lewis, Bradshaw took an evasive step and let fly—only to have Harris unload at just that moment. Of the 70 yards the ball traveled in the air, Bradshaw, knocked cold, witnessed exactly none.

Because of the blitz, Washington had single coverage. "I just ran straight past him," Swann said. "No moves, no fakes, just straight-ahead juice." Squeezing Bradshaw's prayer in stride, he made his fourth catch for a total of 161 yards. Dallas rallied to cut the lead to 21–17, but the Steelers would not be denied. With his grace and acrobatics, Swann had given the Cowboys a headache that would last forever.

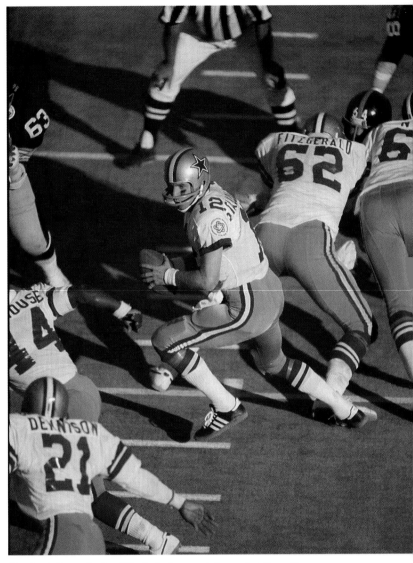

Staubach threw for two TDs, but also was intercepted three times.

For all those gaudy things that happened throughout the afternoon, memories of the 1976 Super Bowl will keep going back to the Pittsburgh Steelers' Lynn Swann climbing into the air like the boy in the Indian rope trick, and coming down with the football. He didn't come down with very many passes last Sunday, really, only four, but he caught the ones that truly mattered. That is why it will seem he spent the day way up there in the crisp sky, a thousand feet above Miami's Orange Bowl, where neither the Dallas Cowboys nor even a squadron of fighter planes could do anything to stop him. When it was all over Lynn Swann and the Steelers had won....

It was Swann soaring above the Cowboys' Mark Washington at the sideline, who fielded a Bradshaw pass of 32 yards and made the drive that put Pittsburgh back in the contest late in the first quarter. Until then Dallas had done everything but cause the Orange Bowl floats to disappear.

—Dan Jenkins
January 26, 1976

COMEBACKS

Two quarterbacks in the shadows: Pity poor Warren Moon (above) whose offense found itself shut down by the suddenly impenetrable Buffalo defense; and Craig Morton (right), whose benching against the 49ers gave Staubach his chance.

OVERVIEW

The plaudits invariably fall to the quarterback. A team is trailing by a couple of touchdowns or more, time is running out, the furious rally begins and when it's over there he is: The man who kept his cool in the face of adversity and directed the decisive march. While it's true that dramatic comebacks always require inspired quarterbacking, ultimately such resurrections demand that other offensive players make play after play, that defensive players make tackle after tackle, that kickers make try after try—that, in fact, the quarterback merely does his part while his teammates do theirs.

When the Buffalo Bills trailed the Houston Oilers 35–3 in the second half of their 1993 AFC playoff game, animated linebacker and all-around free spirit Darryl Talley refused to let his teammates give up, inspiring the Bills' defense to pitch a 28-minute shutout, while wide receiver Andre Reed and backup running back Kenneth Davis helped propel the Bills to TD after TD. When they were finished, Buffalo had pieced together the largest, most amazing comeback in league history.

Another linebacker, the Lions' Joe Schmidt, refused to allow the scoreboard to weaken his resolve as Detroit trailed by 17 in the third quarter

Backup Washington scored two touchdowns to emerge as the surprise star of the Redskins' win over the Raiders, while Tony Hill (left) caught eight passes in Dallas' victory over Washington, including the game-winner.

of a '57 playoff game. Three times the San Francisco 49ers tried to crack Detroit's goal line from inside the 10 to increase their lead to 24; twice Schmidt rose up to stuff them. "That was a minor victory in itself," said coach George Wilson. Thus began a turnaround that propelled Detroit to the NFL championship game and their third title of the decade.

The Washington Redskins had the hated Cowboys on the ropes 17–zip with a postseason berth at stake in 1979. On two occasions huge defensive plays kept the game from getting out of reach—Dallas safety Cliff Harris forced a fumble, and tackle Larry Cole stopped fullback John Riggins on third-and-short— and the Cowboys galloped back to win. Four years

later the Redskins would experience a similar exhilaration against the Los Angeles Raiders, who led 35–20 midway through the fourth quarter. A key block downfield by center Jeff Bostic, an onside kick recovery by Greg Williams and two touchdowns by backup running back Joe Washington put the Skins on top to stay.

The onside kick was a factor, too, in the Cowboys' comeback against the Niners in the 1972 playoffs. It was only after Mel Renfro latched onto Toni Fritsch's squib that Dallas could march to the winning TD and erase what had been a 15-point deficit. The result covered substitute quarterback Roger Staubach in glory, and he was deserving. So, too, were Renfro and Fritsch.

"We had control of this game like no team's ever had control of a game," Houston quarterback Warren Moon recalled of his team's 28–3 halftime lead of an AFC wild-card playoff game in Buffalo. In those 30 minutes, Moon had directed the Oilers' run-and-shoot attack with dead-eye precision, completing 19 of 22 passes for 218 yards and four touchdowns. In the Buffalo locker room, swizzle-stick-gnawing defensive coordinator Walt Corey addressed his shell-shocked troops. "I love you," he told them, "but if you don't start playing, I'll kill you."

Gale Gilbert, the Bills' third-string quarterback, tried to inflate the spirits of second-stringer Frank Reich, who was at the helm in place of a hobbled Jim Kelly. "Hey, you did this in college," Gilbert reminded him. "You can do it here." On Nov. 10, 1984, Reich had engineered the biggest comeback in NCAA Division I history, rallying Maryland from a 31–0 deficit to defeat Miami 42–40. Now he headed back onto the Rich Stadium field reminding himself of what he had learned at school: One play at a time.

But the Bills only fell one play farther behind. Just two minutes into the third quarter Reich threw an interception that Houston safety Bubba McDowell returned 58 yards for a TD. Buffalo trailed 35–3. The Bills had lost 27–3 at Houston in the season finale, so now, over slightly more than six quarters, the Oilers were on a 62–6 roll. On the Bills' bench, star running back Thurman Thomas sat with a hip pointer, All-Pro linebacker Cornelius Bennett was out with a hamstring pull. Two Houston TV reporters in the press box booked nonrefundable plane tickets for the upcoming playoff game in Pittsburgh. In the stands, 10,000 of the 75,141 Buffalo faithful abandoned all hope and exited.

If there was the slightest hope of survival, it hung in the

Prior to coolly directing the Bills' comeback, Reich had thrown only 47 passes during the '92 season.

Reed's third consecutive touchdown put the Bills into the lead for the first time with 3:08 remaining.

The Oilers' leaking, tiring defense had to protect a four-point advantage. Houston immediately forced Buffalo into a third-and-four, but when a pass play was sent in, Reich called time.

"I wanted to know whether we were going to go for it on fourth down if we didn't make it," Reich said. "Marv said we probably would. So I said, if we're going to go for it, why not try to run for it? They won't be expecting it."

There were nods all around, and then Davis took a handoff in the light mist, skated through the

In SI's Words

guard-tackle hole on the right side and sprinted 35 yards to the Houston 33. The crowd went nuts. There was blood in the mist now—it was

the Oilers'—and the Buffalo faithful could smell it. Someone shook the REVENGE IS BEST SERVED COLD sign hanging behind the Houston bench, trying to get the players' attention. But someone else already had their attention: The Oilers couldn't believe what they were seeing from Reich, the unassuming career backup.

—Peter King
January 11, 1993

80

20-mph wind that was now at the Bills' backs. And in Corey's decision to scrap his six-defensive back alignment against Houston's quartet of receivers and return to the Bills' customary 3–4 scheme—"If we were going to go down," Corey said later, "I wanted to go down with our biggest and best people on the field." And in Reich, whose performance had only served to jack up Moon's confidence.

Reich, who had been Kelly's backup for the previous seven years, had attempted only 47 passes during the 1992 season—none for TDs. The Bills, however, still had faith. "It'll take a slow, cerebral approach to win this game," Buffalo wideout Steve Tasker had said before kickoff, "and Frank's as cerebral as they come." *One play at a time.* It took 10, methodically pieced together, for him to march Buffalo 50 yards to paydirt. Thomas's sub, Kenneth Davis, pounded in from a yard out, and with 8:52 left in the third, it was 35–10. *We're still up 25,* Moon thought. *We're fine.*

The Bills recovered an onside kick. Four plays and less than a minute later, Reich lofted a 38-yard bomb to Don Beebe to make it 35–17. Houston's offense went nowhere on three plays. Taking over on his 41, Reich needed only four snaps to score again, connecting with Andre Reed from 26 yards out. Houston 35, Buffalo 24 with 4:21 left in the third. Bills linebacker Darryl Talley exhorted his teammates, slapping backs and screaming, "Believe!" Within seconds, safety Henry Jones had picked off a Moon pass and returned it to the Houston 23. On fourth-and-five, Reich drilled an 18-yard strike to Reed, who had been demanding the ball.

The Oilers led 35–31 with 2:00 to play in the third quarter. "It was like time was standing still," Houston wide receiver Ernest Givins said, "like they were scoring every 15, 20 seconds." The Bills' resilience was riveting TV watchers across the country—except, of course, in the Buffalo area, where the game was blacked out because 5,000 tickets had gone unsold.

Houston took advantage of the wind in the fourth quarter to drive to Buffalo's 14 with seven minutes left. But just as Al Del Greco prepared to kick a 31-yard field goal, the elements rebelled. Rain began to fall, and holder Greg Montgomery couldn't handle the slippery ball and the kick failed. The Oilers' D immediately forced the Bills into a third-and-four on their own 32. Coach Marv Levy ordered up a pass; Reich, noting that they were in four-down territory, lobbied for a run. Levy relented, and Davis rumbled for 35 yards.

Five plays later Reed snatched a 17-yard pass in the end zone. The comeback seemed complete: Buffalo 38, Hous-

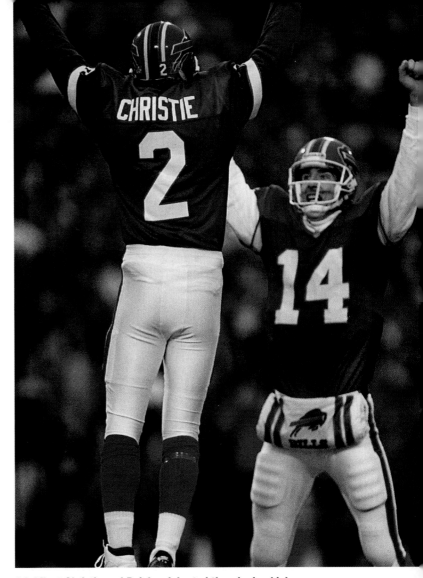

A jubilant Christie and Reich celebrated the winning kick.

ton 35. But Moon would march the Oilers 46 yards, setting up a 26-yard Del Greco field goal that tied the game with 12 seconds left. On the third play of overtime Buffalo cornerback Nate Odomes turned the game back around, picking off a Moon pass in Houston territory. That set up Doug Christie's winning 32-yard kick three plays later.

A procession of dazed Oilers wobbled off the field and toward the locker room. Cornerback Cris Dishman muttered to himself; Moon's chin seemed glued to his chest. "How'd we find a way to lose?" wideout Haywood Jeffires asked. "There can't be any reason for this."

Over the 73-year history of the NFL no team had ever rallied from such a large deficit; the biggest margin overcome in a playoff game had been 20 points. In the triumphant Bills' locker room Reich held his wife, Linda, in a long embrace. "I love you," she said.

"Praise the Lord," said Reich.

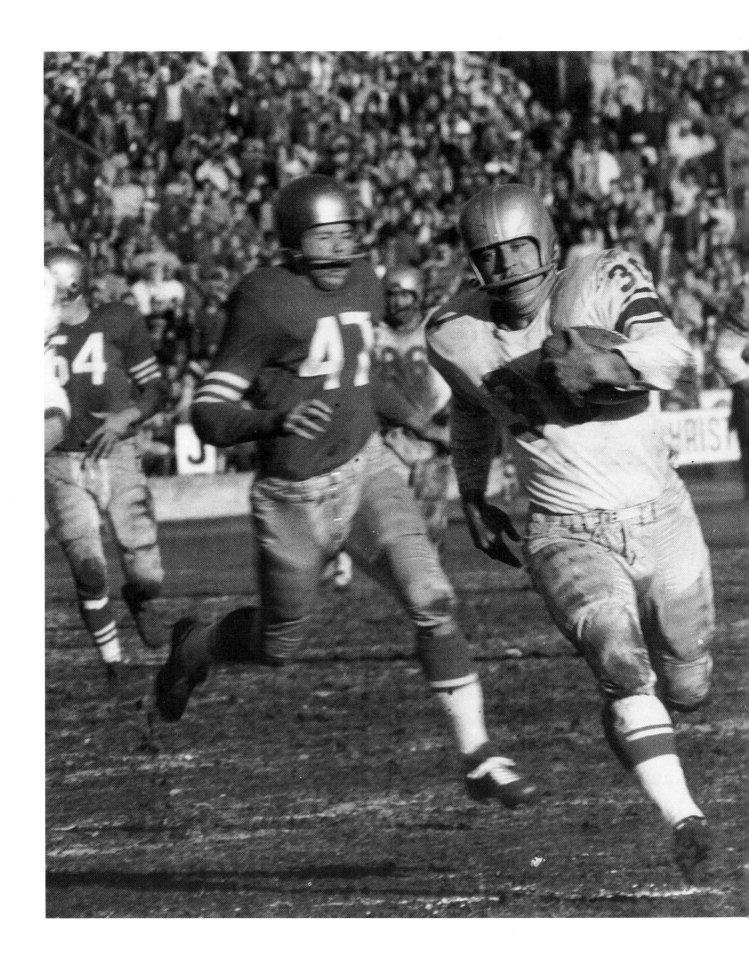

On the first snap of the second half, San Francisco half-back Hugh McElhenny swept right, cut left and sliced 71 zig-zagging yards through the Lions' defense. This play was not the response Detroit coach George Wilson had been looking for when he asked his team at halftime, "What the hell is happening to us?" Nor was it the desired effect of all the Lions' helmet-smashing rage during intermission as they listened to the 49ers gloat on the other side of the locker room wall. Above all, it was not the way to dig out of a 24–7 hole on the road in a do-or-die playoff to reach the NFL championship game.

Then again, Detroit hadn't adhered to anything remotely resembling a standard game plan since two days before the 1957 preseason started. That was when Buddy Parker, who had coached the Lions to two titles, stood up at a boosters' banquet and said, "I have a situation here I cannot handle. This is the worst team in training camp I have ever seen. The material is all right, but the team is dead. I don't want to get involved in another losing season, so I'm leaving Detroit football. I'm leaving tonight." With that, Parker stepped down from the podium and exited his job.

In his place came Wilson, who had been a part-time Lions assistant, part-time mill supplies salesman. After a 3–3 start, he showed his coaching and pitchman skills with comeback after comeback as the Lions won five of their last six games. One triumph had come only a week before, against the Chicago Bears, when Wilson's halftime oratory stirred the Lions from 10 down to a 21–13 victory that clinched their Western Conference playoff spot. He railed again at San Francisco's Kezar Stadium. "You guys are quitters," he told his players. "We've totally given up out there."

The pear-shaped Tracy rolled 58 yards to score the TD that brought the Lions within six.

Detroit's Steve Junker caught eight passes for 92 yards, including a critical 36-yarder during the winning drive.

But team president Edwin J. Anderson took a more sanguine view. "We haven't had a break yet," he said softly to Wilson.

That much was true. In the first quarter, Niners quarterback Y.A. Tittle and flanker R.C. Owens had made their "alley oop" connection for a 34-yard touchdown, and McElhenny had raced 48 yards for another score. Detroit's offense, meanwhile, had clanked and sputtered like a Motor City lemon behind a couple of backups: fullback Tom (the Bomb) Tracy, who was filling in for John Henry Johnson, and quarterback Tobin Rote, who had started in place of injured Bobby Layne. In the first half the subs had scraped together all of 107 yards. Through the locker room wall, the Lions could hear the Niners rattling on about what cars they were going to buy with their winning shares. Near the end of intermission the P.A. announcer informed the 60,180 fans that tickets to the championship game were now on sale.

Then came Hurrying Hugh's 71-yard jaunt to Detroit's nine. To echo Parker, the material was all right, but the team was dead.

Detroit's D was the first unit to show signs of life. Three times the 49ers tried to cross the goal line, but linebacker Joe Schmidt and Co. refused to crack. San Francisco settled for a Gordy Saltau field goal. "It was 27–7 and that

84

Owens went skyward to score the game's opening TD for the 49ers.

didn't look good at all," Wilson said. "But because we'd finally shown some spirit, I thought things were getting better. We just needed someone to make a big play."

On the next series, Tittle fumbled, linebacker Bob Long recovered at the 49ers' 27 and Tracy came up huge. Nine plays later, Tracy, a 5'9", 210-pound, pear-shaped fullback with a bristle cut, bowled in from the two to make it 27–14. Within a minute, the Bomb struck again. This time he took off around right end, reversed his field, slipped—ducked under, that is—several tackles and rolled 58 yards for another score. Detroit trailed by six.

The Niners punted, and Rote steered the Lions 54 yards on five plays to their third TD with confidence and precision. Halfback Gene Gedman went in from the two and Jim Martin's extra point gave them the lead, 28–27. In less than 4½ minutes Detroit had scored three touchdowns to overcome a 17-point deficit. There was only one catch: The Lions had 14 minutes to protect their one-point advantage.

The breaks Anderson had been counting on took care of that. On each of the 49ers' next four possessions, a different Lion dispossessed them of the ball. The last was defensive tackle Roger Zatkoff, who made the first interception of his pro career in the game's final minute. In the end, it was hard to say whether Wilson, Tracy, Rote, or none of them was most responsible for motivating the Lions. "We realized," offensive tackle Lou Creekmur said, "that our championship playoff money was going right down the drain."

Tobin Rote led the NFL in passing in 1956 as a starter for the Green Bay Packers, but it was as a backup for the Detroit Lions that he attained his career peak. Filling in for the injured Bobby Layne, he led Detroit's memorable comeback over San Francisco in the Western Conference playoff, then topped that performance the following week in the NFL title game against the Browns. No comeback was necessary as the Lions jumped out to a 17–0 first-quarter lead en route to a 59–14 shellacking. Rote ran for a touchdown in the first quarter and passed for four more, including a 78-yarder to Jim Doran in the third. A 6'2", 211-pound Texan with great versatility, Rote remained with Detroit until 1959, then moved to the Toronto Argonauts. After leading the CFL in passing for three years, he resurfaced with San Diego in 1963 and took the Chargers to the AFL championship, topping the new league with a 59.4 completion percentage. Rote returned to the AFL title game in 1964, losing to Buffalo. He retired two years later as a Denver Bronco.

SPOTLIGHT

35 / 34
COWBOYS / REDSKINS

The funeral wreath spiraled through the Washington dressing room, where huge men sat wiping tears from their bowed faces. The floral arrangement came courtesy of Dallas defensive end Harvey Martin, who had received it from an anonymous fan before the teams' regular-season finale at Texas Stadium. Now it ricocheted off a locker, gashed the knee of placekicker Mark Moseley and lay at the feet of the vanquished Redskins, whose playoff hopes had just been laid to rest in the last 140 seconds of the game. "They might as well take it home with them," Martin said. "They're the ones who need it. They're dead."

Martin was merely delivering the oration; the *coup de grace* had come courtesy of the Cowboys' 37-year-old quarterback, Roger Staubach. Sixteen years removed from his Heisman Trophy–winning season at Navy but still a nice guy to have in a pinch, Staubach had slayed Washington with his usual weapons—unwavering confidence and an unerring right arm that completed 24 of 42 passes for 336 yards and three touchdowns. That this comeback would take place against the Cowboys' staunchest rival made victory sweet. That it would exact revenge for a bitter loss earlier in the season made it Staubach's greatest Lazarus act ever.

On Nov. 18 at RFK Stadium, Washington coach Jack Pardee had sent Moseley in to kick a 24-yard field goal with his team up 31–20 and 14 seconds remaining. Pardee's rationale: He might need that extra three-spot to gain an edge in the tiebreaking system used to determine the playoff teams. But that thinking didn't wash with the Cowboys, who felt the Skins were rubbing salt in their wounds. Nerves were further frayed on the charter flight back to Dallas when some Cowboys could actually be

heard laughing. "Used to be when Dallas lost to Washington you could hear a pin drop," Martin fumed. "If you don't hurt when you lose, you're gonna lose again."

The following day Dallas coach Tom Landry made a calculated cut, releasing linebacker Thomas (Hollywood) Henderson. The Cowboys won their next two games to clinch a spot in the playoffs. The Redskins had all but qualified for the postseason, too. After finishing 8–8 in '78 they were 10–5; even if the Redskins lost at Dallas, Chicago would have to beat the St. Louis Cardinals by 31 points to edge Washington out for the final NFC spot. The Bears hadn't scored more than 35 in a game all year.

All that was at stake, then, was the NFC East title and an old score. In the Cowboys' meeting room, one word had been written on the chalkboard and underlined three times: ATTITUDE. On the field for the pregame coin toss, the Redskins' captains offered their hands to Staubach and defensive tackle Diron Talbert. Their hands were rejected.

The lead was treated with similar

Hill's game-winning catch, on a feathery toss from Staubach, came with 42 seconds remaining in the game.

disdain. Washington responded to the 'Boys-will-be-boys snub by scoring 17 straight points, capped by a 55-yard pass from Joe Theismann to running back Benny Malone, the Redskins' longest scoring play from scrimmage all season. But Staubach's unshaken hand held some answers. He took the Cowboys on 70- and 85-yard TD drives, and by the first possession of the third quarter they led 21–17.

Back came the Redskins to take control, 27–21. Then, on what appeared to be a botched play, Washington had a new longest scoring play from scrimmage: Fullback John Riggins cut right and sprinted down the sideline for a 66-yard TD. With 5:21 to play, the Redskins were up 34–21, with the ball. Then they were without it. Safety Cliff Harris forced running back Clarence Harmon to fumble, and Randy White recovered on the Cowboys' 41-yard line with 3:49 to go. Said Staubach, "It was an opportunity that had 'Last One Available' stamped all over it."

The usually unstoppable Riggins was tackled short of the goal line on this first quarter touchdown try.

Roger the Dodger knew a bit about seizing opportunity. As a Dallas starter he had presided over 21 come-from-behind wins, though he had never rallied the team from 17 down. Three straight completions later—the last a 26-yarder to running back Ron Springs down the middle—Dallas had cut the lead to 34–28 with 2:20 remaining. After tackle Larry Cole stopped Riggins cold on third-and-two, Washington punted. With 1:46 left, Dallas took over on its own 25.

Pardee was in a quandary. "If we blitzed we risked letting Roger break one," he would say later. "But if we stood back, he was finding the open guy." Staubach fired (20 yards to wideout Tony Hill); misfired; fired (22 to running back Preston Pearson); misfired; fired (25 to Pearson); misfired. On second-and-goal from the eight, he called Hot Left 17, a throw to the tight end. The Skins blitzed four. Staubach adjusted and floated a pass that landed softly on Hill's fingertips in the right corner of the end zone. "It was a great call by a great quarterback," said cornerback Lemar Parrish, who was covering on the play. "There wasn't much I could do. The throw was perfect."

Rafael Septien's extra point made it 35–34 with 39 seconds left. Some Redskins scanned the scoreboard and saw an even more deflating set of figures: The Bears had won 42–6. "The Lord giveth and He can take it away in a hurry," Pardee said. "That's the only way to understand what took place here." That and Staubach.

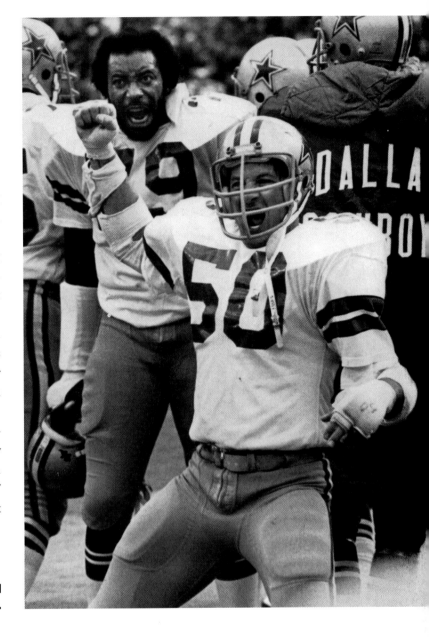

Linebacker D.D. Lewis (50) and Martin celebrated yet another Staubach-engineered miracle comeback.

"I used to dread the ball being hit to me when the game was tight," Roger Staubach's father once said to his son after watching him compete in a high school baseball game in Cincinnati. "You seem to relish it." Like all the great ones, Staubach did indeed relish those moments when the pressure was highest. John Elway may currently occupy the throne as King of the Comeback, but Staubach wore

SPOTLIGHT

that crown first. Staubach engineered 23 fourth-quarter rallies in his 11-year career, but perhaps his most impressive comeback was from a five-year layoff while fulfilling his military obligation as a graduate of the Naval Academy. Though he had graduated from Annapolis in 1964, he didn't take his first pro snap as a starter until 1971, at the age of 29. But Staubach barely missed a beat, leading Dallas to an 11–3 season, winning the NFL Player of the Year Award and quarterbacking a 24–3 rout of Miami in the Super Bowl. Staubach would return to the big game three more times, and when he retired after the 1979 season, he was the highest-rated passer of all time.

REDSKINS / RAIDERS
37 / 35

Raiders managing partner Al Davis could not supress a smile when espousing his pet philosophy: Just win, baby. His team, the Pride-and-Poise boys, the snarling silver-and-black, had just overhauled the Redskins at RFK Stadium. Down 17–7 at halftime, Los Angeles had rallied to take a 35–20 lead with 7:31 to go in the game. Davis reveled as if this were his finest hour, and so it seemed—for the moment.

Washington not only had 54,016 of the most ardent fans in the league on hand to provide inspiration, but also had the firepower to come back. In slightly more than two seasons with the Redskins, coach Joe Gibbs had developed an amalgam of weapons—the Hogs, who rooted out holes for fullback John Riggins, the Fun Bunch, who made circus catches from scrambling Joe Theismann, and terrific special teams. Now, did the 3–1 Redskins have enough pride and poise, not to mention chutzpah, to out-Raider the 4–0 Raiders?

Most important, could Washington win without Riggins? Even with a sore back he had rambled for 91 yards and a touchdown on 26 carries. "Riggo right, Riggo left, Riggo out the door," said tackle George Starke of the behemoth Hogs' favorite game plan. But with the Skins needing to score quickly, Gibbs called Riggo to the sidelines. In his place came 30-year-old journeyman Joe Washington, who had carried the ball only 23 times in the first four games after undergoing surgery on both knees during the offseason. Washington hardly fit the porcine mold: At 5'10" and 179 pounds, he was four inches shorter and 51 pounds lighter than Riggins.

The Raiders had shown their pride—and depth—earlier in the game. On their only score of the first half, wide receiver Cliff Branch pulled a hamstring while racing 99

Brown snared the TD pass that brought the Redskins within eight, then made three critical catches in the game-winning drive.

90

Theismann was outstanding, throwing for 417 yards, 190 of them on the last three drives.

with the play-action threat of Riggins. He now carried the burden on his shoulders, which frequently had been planted in the turf by a Hog-tying Raiders line that had six sacks. Said L.A. defensive end Howie Long, who had four of them, "It was the longest, hardest football game I ever played in."

On the Redskins first snap Theismann flipped a screen pass to Washington, who got a ferocious block from center Jeff Bostic on 6'7" linebacker Ted Hendricks. "I just saw the big s.o.b. coming and decided to take half of him and Joe could have the other half," Bostic said. Washington accepted that split and scooted 67 yards to the Raiders 21. Three snaps later, Theismann found Charlie Brown on an 11-yard TD that sliced the lead to 35–27.

Los Angeles readied for an onside kick by putting nine players up front. Washington special teams coach Wayne Sevier instructed Jeff Hayes to try a "power kick" through the first wave of receivers. "We have it on our list of kicks," Sevier said, "but we never got around to practicing it." Without practice Hayes was perfect, drilling a liner that deflected off one of the chorus line of 18 Raider legs. Greg Williams recovered for the Redskins on the L.A. 32. After settling for Mark Moseley's 34-yard field goal, Washington trailed 35–30.

A pair of stops by linebacker Neal Olkewicz helped force a Raiders punt with 1:50 to go. Theismann had 69 yards to travel against a soft zone defense that lacked its two starting safeties. He rifled three straight passes to Brown for nine, 26 and 28 yards, respectively, streaking to the L.A. six with 33 seconds left. On second down the Raiders shifted to their normal man-to-man. The Redskins split Washington, the lone back, outside left tackle in order to draw coverage from a linebacker. L.A.'s Rod Martin tried to jam him at the line, but Washington skimmed off and darted inside. Theismann's lob over Martin's outstretched hands was high, but Washington rose to the occasion and snatched the lead for good, 37–35.

The Skins had reeled off 17 straight points thanks to Theismann, who in three scoring drives connected on nine of 12 passes for 190 yards. "One for the history books," Theismann called it.

It's not known whether Davis was contemplating history at the end of the game. But he could be seen up in the press box, tearing a piece of paper into tiny scraps and staring into space.

yards with a pass from Jim Plunkett. Enter Calvin Muhammad, who scorched the Skins with two second-half touchdown grabs. Plunkett tossed two yards to tight end Todd Christensen for a third TD. Even when L.A. lost its poise there was a payoff: Greg Pruitt mistakenly fielded a punt on his own three-yard line, then went the distance to make it 35–20.

With 7:20 left in the game, Theismann took over after the kickoff on his own 12-yard line. He had been so-so thus far, completing 12 of 27 passes for 227 yards, but that was

Washington, a backup to Riggins, ran four times for only 10 yards, but made his mark with the game-winning catch.

From his own 31 Theismann moved the Skins steadily goalward, and in just five plays he had his touchdown—on a six-yard flip to Washington over the middle with 33 seconds left. Three of those plays were completions of nine, 26 and 28 yards to Brown, who took advantage of L.A.'s alleged prevent defense. Both his long gainers were on elementary "in" patterns that struck uncustomarily deep in the Raider zone. "They played a soft zone and we just picked it," said Brown.

Near the goal line, however, the Raiders went back to man-to-man.

In SI's Words

The Redskins lined up in a strange formation—Washington was the lone back but he was stationed outside his left tackle. The Skins can run out of the formation, but it's basically designed to get Washington isolated on a linebacker—and that's just what happened. L.A.'s Rod Martin tried to chuck him at the line, but Washington skimmed off, went inside and took Theismann's lob over Martin's outstretched hands for the touchdown that ended one of the most spectacular comebacks in Redskin history.

—Jack McCallum
October 10, 1983

94

In the third preseason game of 1972, Roger (the Dodger) Staubach smacked into Rams linebacker Marlin McKeever. The collision not only separated Staubach's right shoulder but also loosened his grip on the Cowboys' starting quarterback job, which he had finally wrested from Craig Morton. Most of Dallas's offensive players preferred Morton's experience; the guys on D liked Staubach's fiery style. Coach Tom Landry had been so unsure that he had the pair alternate *snaps* in 1970, but Staubach took charge in '71, going 9–0 as a starter and winning the NFC Player of the Year award.

Now he would be out of action for at least two months. "What made Roger try to run over McKeever," Landry said, "is what will bring him back."

Staubach did return in Week 5, but Dallas was clicking with Morton, who wound up completing a team record 185 passes during the regular season and was voted Most Popular Cowboy by the fans. The 30-year-old Staubach pitched here and there in relief. While that was hardly the role he wanted, it was one he accepted with characteristic dignity, evincing nothing but respect for the battle-scarred Morton. "If I had two operations on my throwing arm," Staubach said, "I'd be a cook on a Navy ship somewhere right now."

But in the Cowboys' playoff opener against the 49ers at Candlestick Park, Morton's directional guidance system was off. Midway through the third quarter he had connected on just eight of 21 throws for 96 yards, and set up a pair of San Francisco TDs by tossing an interception and coughing up a fumble. The 49ers were in command, 28–13, and the scent of victory was particularly sweet. Dallas had bounced the Niners from the postseason the last two years.

After missing most of the season due to injury, Staubach returned to the fray with another trademark comeback.

95

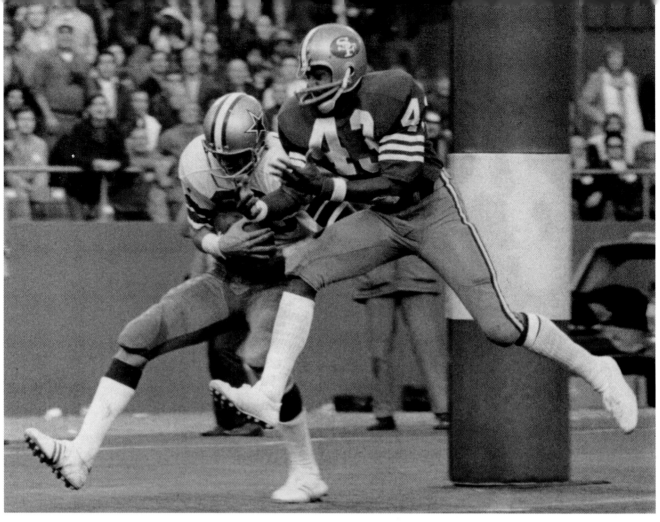

Hall (43) was just a split second late on the rifle throw from Staubach to Sellers that won the game for Dallas.

Landry, looking for a spark, told Staubach to warm up. "Bring him on," shouted defensive end Cedric Hardman from the San Francisco sideline. "He's not gonna make any difference today." Initially the Dodger didn't. Staubach's first pass was incomplete, and Hardman and Co. were teeing off; they would force one fumble and sack Staubach four times in the next 10 minutes. But he wasn't about to wilt under the pressure. Said Dallas tight end Mike Ditka, "Roger Staubach is a man that you can't ever tell he can't do something."

After the Niners' Bruce Gossett blew a 25-yard field goal, the Cowboys came to life. A draw play to Calvin Hill picked up 48 yards and set up Toni Fritsch's third field goal of the day, cutting the lead to 28–16 with 8:58 left in the fourth quarter. The 61,214 fans grew edgy, sensing that their team had lost some of its offensive aggression. In the second half the Niners would fail to convert six third downs. On four of them, they ran.

Once again San Francisco's kicking game gave Dallas a break. A 17-yard punt by McCann set the Cowboys up at their own 45 with 1:53 to go. Two completions later,

Staubach had them on the 20, where the Niners mounted an all-out rush. "But he read—or guessed—our double-blitz," San Francisco coach Dick Nolan said. Wide receiver Billy Parks beat man-to-man coverage on a post pattern, and Staubach winged it in. The Cowboys trailed by five, but they had only one timeout and 1:30 left.

Fritsch would have to try an onside kick. He sent a twisting, turning squib toward wide receiver Preston Riley, who lost the handle as he got hit. "All I saw was the football on the ground," Dallas cornerback Mel Renfro said. "I grabbed it and hung on for dear life."

At midfield, the Cowboys had possession again.

Wary of Staubach's scrambling, the San Francisco D hadn't allowed him to escape the pocket. Until now. Unable to find an open receiver, Staubach ran down the middle for 21 yards. With only 56 seconds remaining, he faded back and fired to Parks near the sideline for 19 more. Dallas was on the 10-yard line when flanker Ron Sellers told Staubach he could get open on a curl over the middle. Staubach called 62 Wing Sideline—a pass to

The Cowboys had reason to celebrate after coming back from a 15-point fourth quarter deficit.

Parks—but he told Sellers that he would be the hot receiver in case San Francisco blitzed again.

The Niners did indeed send a linebacker. Windlan Hall, a rookie safety who had played brilliantly, was in single coverage on Sellers. "I threw the ball as hard as I could," Staubach said. And as accurately. Hall was a split second late and the Cowboys, once down by 15, went out in front. Staubach had completed 12 of 20 passes for 174 yards and two TDs.

Quarterback John Brodie marched the Niners all the way to the Dallas 22, but a holding penalty nullified their last big gain. "You can never say a game is in the bag," Brodie said. "But this one looked awfully good." Until the Cowboys pulled their familiar quarterback shuffle. "Roger has this way about him," Landry said. "He can turn things around."

AFTERMATH

Having played on the same side in Super Bowls V and VI, Staubach and Morton faced off against each other in Supe XII—Staubach as a Cowboy and Morton as a Bronco. The Cowboys defense rode the Broncos hard out of the pen and Morton was intercepted four times—completing just four of 15 passes for 39 yards—before being retired early in the third quarter. Second stringer Norris Weese had no better luck trying to buck the Orange Crush, which held him to less than 50 yards total. Staubach in the meantime connected on 17 of 25 passes, including a 45-yard TD throw to Butch Johnson. By the end of the day, the Cowboys had hobbled the overachieving Broncos in a 27–10 rout. Morton played out his career in Denver without making another Super Bowl appearance. Staubach tried unsuccessfully to win another Super Bowl against Pittsburgh the following year; he retired after the 1979 season and was elected to the Hall of Fame in 1985.

NAIL-BITERS

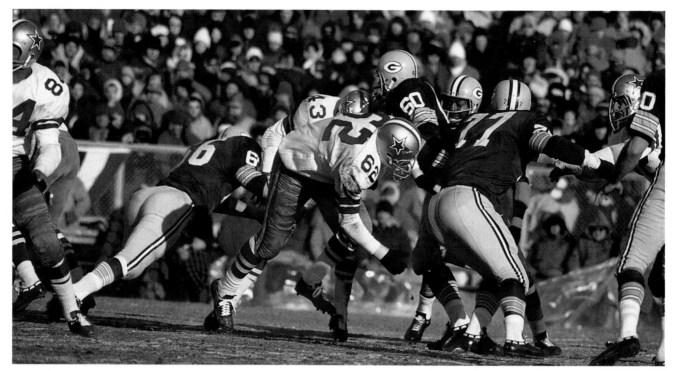

The frozen turf of Lambeau Field (above) was the harsh setting for the Ice Bowl, one of the tensest games in NFL history; New York's Jeff Hostetler (right) led the Giants' throwback offense to victory in Super Bowl XXV.

OVERVIEW

Imagine for a moment that NBC had not chosen to cut away from the last minutes of the AFL grudgefest between the New York Jets and the Oakland Raiders in 1968. Imagine instead that many of the most interested viewers would have been allowed to *see* the two touchdowns scored in the span of nine seconds that reversed the teams' fortunes. Would that game have qualified as a nail-biter? No. What frays fans' nerves is *anticipation*; the preemptive appearance of the goat-herding Swiss orphan named Heidi on TV screens, rather than the game, was what made the tension unbearable.

Very few moments in pro football history have been more gripping than the conclusion of the Ice Bowl of 1967. The champion Green Bay Packers had one play with which to stave off their heirs apparent, the Dallas Cowboys. The temperature in Green Bay was a record low; the turf at Lambeau Field a sheet of ice. Could the Pack, among the most reliable running teams in NFL history, advance two feet to victory?

Two words are enough to drive any fan into a frenzy: sudden death. Not only are they dire in themselves, but they also signify high stakes—a regular-season game can end in a tie, but a playoff game cannot. Twice in a decade the Miami Dolphins' season came down to one scoring play; in both cases the play hinged on the instep of one of the smallest men on the field. After an exhausting

Winslow's superhuman peformance against the Dolphins included a block (above) of Miami's potential game-winning field goal; while the nation watched *Heidi*, Oakland's Charlie Smith (23, left) scored the game-winner against the Jets.

performance by San Diego Chargers tight end Kellen Winslow and a gritty comeback directed by Dolphins backup quarterback Don Strock, which of the teams' placekickers, each of whom had missed earlier field goals, would come through?

On Christmas Day in 1971, the same question hung in the unusually warm Kansas City evening, when the Chiefs' Jan Stenerud and Garo Yepremian traded shots for glory. Could Yepremian—erstwhile washout, part-time tie-painter and happy-go-lucky card player—trump the kicker who had beaten him out for the Pro Bowl?

Only two Super Bowls have come down to a field-goal try in the waning seconds. In '91, the offenses of the Buffalo Bills and the New York Giants were the yin and yang of the NFL: the former a no-hud-dle, air-it-out, modern-day model; the latter a slow-down, grind-it-out throwback. Their clash was made all the more riveting by the teams' sharp execution, and it almost made sense that the winner would be decided by the closest thing to a coin toss. Buffalo's Scott Norwood had connected on a 47-yarder during the season, his longest kick that year. Did he have one more in him?

Detroit quarterback Bobby Layne was made for such moments, when the chips were down and toughness and ingenuity counted most. The Lions trailed the Cleveland Browns 16–10, and the NFL title was at stake. Could Layne, with his star receiver sidelined, pitch Detroit to the title? Would Cleveland coach Paul Brown lose once again to the Lions? Even Heidi would have found it hard to watch.

December 31, 1967

Right guard Jerry Kramer ambled from the Green Bay huddle to the line of scrimmage under the haze of his own breath. Center Ken Bowman, having slipped on the frigid turf the previous two plays, lowered himself anxiously over the ball. Left guard Gale Gillingham planted his right fingertips on the ground, disregarding the numbness in his hand. The heart of the Packers' offensive line—ice-cold, bone-weary, and oft-manhandled by Dallas's Doomsday Defense—braced itself for one last play, to clear a path wide enough for a 24-inch run that would preserve a dynasty. Welcome to the Ice Bowl.

Shortly after Cowboy defensive tackle Bob Lilly woke up on the day of the NFL Championship Game, he threw a cup of water against the window of his Green Bay hotel room. The water froze on the glass.

The temperature outside was minus-13. This was the coldest Dec. 31 in the city's history. At Lambeau Field, a heating system installed six inches under the sod that was supposed to generate 750,000 volts of heat malfunctioned the minute the tarp was removed. The ground froze.

Referee Norm Schachter and his crew, outfitted in thermal gear they had bought that morning, would be unable to blow their whistles all afternoon. The wooden balls inside them froze.

The unprecedented cold, whipped by a 15 mph crosswind, was somehow fitting for an epic clash between one franchise clinging to supremacy and the other just one play from snatching it away. On Jan. 1 the previous season,

**Starr's one-yard sneak was classic Packer football:
When in doubt, keep things as simple as possible.**

104

A pair of Starr-to-Dowler passes put Green Bay in front 14–0 in the second quarter.

eight times for 76 yards, with one of those hits producing a fumble that Cowboys end George Andrie picked up and gingerly carried into the end zone. Another bobble on a punt return by Willie Wood set up a Danny Villanueva field goal, and early in the fourth quarter Dan Reeves shocked the Pack secondary with a 50-yard halfback option pass to Lance Rentzel. "Oh my Lord," cried beaten Green Bay cornerback Bob Jeter. "What have I done?"

Trailing 17–14, Starr took over with 4:50 left and the ball on the Packers' 31. He chipped away with the short stuff—a screen pass to stalwart halfback Donny Anderson, a handoff to fullback Chuck Mercein, the former Yale star who had been bought off waivers that year for the whopping sum of $100. When Green Bay reached midfield, Dallas dropped back deeper in coverage to protect against a big gain. So Starr, frosty but unflappable, kept throwing to his backs instead. Gillingham suckered Lilly on a draw play, and Mercein shot through the hole to the three. Anderson rushed for a first down, then twice more, blasting just inside the one-yard line. With 16 seconds left, Starr spent his last timeout.

Under the jerry-rigged canvas dugout that covered the Packer bench, Lombardi weighed his options. An 18-yard field goal would tie it. A pass into the end zone could win it; if incomplete, it would at least stop the clock with time

Green Bay had squeezed past Dallas 34–27 at the Cotton Bowl, thanks to defensive back Tom Brown, who picked off Don Meredith's last-down pass to seal the Pack's second straight title. No team in the 35-year history of the Championship Game had won three in a row. Green Bay would be trying to make history in the sort of harsh conditions coach Vince Lombardi fell to his knees and prayed for. "Vince stayed down a little bit too long on this one," defensive tackle Henry Jordan would say afterward.

Quarterback Bart Starr, whose two TD throws to split end Boyd Dowler would stake Green Bay to a 14–0 lead, spent much of the day prostrate as well. Dallas sacked him

The Green Bay Packers of the 1960s were such a dominant, well-oiled unit that individual players tended to be underappreciated cogs in the machine, overshadowed by its total efficiency. This was especially true in the case of quarterback Bart Starr. A 17th-round draft pick out of the University of Alabama in 1956, Starr didn't get his chance to shine until Vince Lombardi took over the Pack in

'59. The team had gone 1-10-1 in 1958 and Starr was anything but on the rise, watching much of the action from the bench. But Lombardi liked

SPOTLIGHT

Starr's mechanics. Lombardi also saw an intelligent, disciplined leader around whom he could build a team. Indeed, he built a dynasty, and Starr

became his general. Assuming the starting QB job in 1960, Starr led the team to a division title. The Pack would win five more that decade as well as NFL titles in '61 and '62, and three straight from 1965–67. After the '66 and '67 triumphs, the Packers went on to vanquish the AFL champions in Super Bowls I and II. Their steady quarterback was named MVP of both games.

A crowd of 50,861 hardy souls braved the minus-13-degree temperatures to watch one of the NFL's alltime classics.

for one more play. The footing near that goal line was particularly treacherous. Starr said he could sneak in. Lombardi, loathe to risk a kick and constitutionally inclined to take the most basic approach, snapped, "Then let's do it and get the hell out of here."

Starr called the play in the huddle: Wedge 30. He ordered up a quick count, too, so that the Cowboys might not be able to dig in. Kramer, miraculously finding a soft spot in the turf for a toehold, hoped that Cowboy tackle Jethro Pugh would raise up on the snap, as Kramer had seen him do on film, so that he could knock him off balance. Lilly, lowered in his stance, silently wished the play would come his way. Reporters hacked away at the frost

on the press box windows as 50,861 fans cocooned in wool stood to watch.

The sequence has been replayed untold times, encapsulating as it does the essences of Lombardi, the Packers and the hand-to-hand combat over inches of turf that is football. Kramer timed the snap beautifully and blasted off the line. Pugh rose slightly, and Bowman and Kramer plowed into him. Starr slipped between their blocks and lunged into the end zone. Later, a thawed Lombardi expressed his appreciation for all the grit and will and well-oiled execution under pressure that went into that moment. "This was it," he said of Green Bay's third championship. "This was our greatest one."

CHARGERS / DOLPHINS

41 / 38

More amazing than the endless stream of completions by San Diego's Dan Fouts and Miami's 24-point comeback behind a second-string quarterback and the touchdown that looked like something drawn up on someone's palm on a sandlot and the three missed field goals that each could have decided the AFC divisional playoff and the winning kick by Rolf Benirschke that brought to an end the most breathtaking rollercoaster ride of a 74-minute game in NFL history—more amazing than all of that was this: Just days before the kickoff there were questions about Kellen Winslow's dependability.

At 6' 5" and 242 pounds, Winslow was called a tight end by convenience, there being no easy way to sum up his roles of tight end, wide receiver, fullback, wingback and slotback. He had speed and size and grace and the sort of unmatched gifts that made the Chargers' attack unique and unstoppable. He addressed the questions about his dependability at a pre-game press conference. "They call me the sissy, the San Diego chicken," he told reporters. "I'm the tight end who won't block. They say I need a heart transplant. In fact, our whole team has no heart."

Then he added, "But I'm very self-confident. I know what I can do. I know what our team can do."

Winslow could never have guessed what this game would demand of him. He took oxygen to battle the humidity and 87-degree heat at the Orange Bowl. Each hit he gave or took aggravated the pinched nerve in his left shoulder. Time and again he had to be carried off the field because of cramps in his back and legs. In the locker room after the game his lip was bleeding and his left eye was swollen as he talked about his playoff-record 13 catches

Wes Chandler's 56-yard punt return put the Chargers ahead 14–0 in the first quarter.

Benirschke's 29-yard field goal finally ended the marathon contest with 13:52 elapsed in overtime.

for 166 yards and his field-goal block that had made victory possible.

San Diego coach Don Coryell had worried about the debilitating heat. At 8 p.m. on New Year's Eve he had dispatched the team's business manager to round up eight dozen bananas, hoping the potassium they contained would help his players avoid cramping. Miami coach Don Shula, meanwhile, had a more substantial concern: how his defensive backs, whom one local columnist had given the "turkeys of the year award," would hold up under an all-out assault from Air Coryell. "We can't let San Diego have anything quick," said Shula, "anything cheap."

The Chargers proceeded to grab the lead quickly (24–zip in the first 13:29) and cheaply (via a fumble on a kickoff and an interception). Shula replaced his 23-year-old quarterback, David Woodley, with eight-year veteran Don Strock, and the Miami attack began to click. "You could sense the difference," said San Diego linebacker Linden King. "Strock had a real presence out there." He guided Miami to a field goal, then a TD. With 30 seconds left in the half, the Dolphins got the ball back at midfield; 23 seconds later Strock had them at the San Diego 25.

To a skeptical Miami huddle Strock relayed Shula's call: 87 Circle Curl Lateral. It began with a button-hook to receiver Duriel Harris 15 yards downfield. "All we wanted to do was let him catch it and converge on him," said Willie Buchanan, one of three Charger defensive backs angling to

Winslow (80) had a near-death experience in the hot Miami night.

make the tackle. "Then out of the corner of my eye I saw a guy flying by me." Tony Nathan had looped out of the Miami backfield and taken Harris's lateral untouched down the right sideline. The Dolphins had cut the lead to 24–17 at halftime

Through the rest of regulation the teams resembled heavy-weights looking for a knockout, trading touchdowns like hay-makers. Strock tied the game at 24–all with 4:10 gone in the third quarter on his second scoring pass to tight end Joe Rose. Fouts hit Winslow on a 25-yarder (31–24, San Diego); Strock connected with tight end Bruce Hardy for 50 (31–all); Nathan scampered 12 yards after a Lyle Blackwood intercep-tion (38–31, Miami); running back James Brooks snagged a nine-yarder from Fouts with 58 seconds to play (38–all).

To complete what would have been the greatest come-back in NFL playoff history, Strock drove Miami to the San Diego 26, setting up a 43-yard field goal attempt by Uwe von Schamann with four second left in regulation. Winslow lined up between the tackles and he asked them for a push. He was not normally a member of a San Diego field-goal defense, which had blocked just one kick during the sea-son. The snap was high, the kick low. Winslow swatted it away with his right hand. "The biggest thrill of my life," he said afterward. "I felt like I scored three touchdowns."

Benirschke hooked a 27-yard chip shot in overtime, then Leroy Jones deflected a 34-yard try by von Schamann. Finally, Fouts (33 of 53 for a playoff-record 433 yards) led a 70-yard advance to place Benirscke at the 19, and with 13:52 elapsed in sudden death, he didn't miss. "Thank God it's over," said a spent Winslow to the two Chargers who helped him off the field. "It's the closest to death I've ever been."

DOLPHINS / CHIEFS

27 / 24

When the longest game in NFL history ended at 6:24 p.m. on Christmas Day, one of the most self-contained signal callers in league history began cracking up, laughing at the Kansas City night sky like Mr. Magoo on a bender. Bob Griese got giddy because of the stakes (a berth in the AFC Championship Game) and the playing time (82 minutes and 40 seconds) and overall duration of the game (three hours and 21 minutes). And because of Garo Yepremian.

During five-and-a-half quarters in which Chiefs running back Ed Podolak rolled up a sublime 350 yards of total offense and Griese threw for 263 yards, Yepremian, a placekicker and would-be tackler, loomed over the outcome like a bald, 5' 8" colossus. When the Dolphins returned to Miami near midnight, 17,000 fans greeted them at the airport. A phalanx of policeman tried vainly to protect the 27-year-old Yepremian from his admirers. "It's O.K.," he told the cops, "I love this. Today I am the happiest man. Can you believe this?"

Yepremian was a Yiddish-spewing Cypriot and former club soccer player who kicked off in the first NFL game he saw, for the Detroit Lions in 1966. The following year the Lions cut him. Yepremian sought refuge in his basement, huddling in shame while trying to turn a profit from his pastime: painting neckties. Miami rescued Yepremian from his misery in 1970, and a year later the left instep of his size-seven soccer boot scored a league-leading 117 points. Of his layoff, Yepremian, whose wife affectionately called him the Worm, said, "I am really better off, because I know what happens to a person when he is up and gets knocked down."

Kansas City and Miami had both finished the regular season 10-3-1, but the reigning Super Bowl champion Chiefs had won the teams' six previous meetings by a combined score of 183–47, including four shutouts. Many regarded K.C.'s personnel as the best in the league, and their linebacking corps, headed by Willie Lanier in the middle, was especialy fearsome. "It's one thing to run against a grizzly bear," Dolphins fullback Larry Csonka said, "but when he's a *smart* grizzly bear...."

At kickoff something odd was in the air: The temperature in Kansas City was a balmy 63 degrees. The Chiefs jumped to a 10–0 first-quarter lead on Jan Stenerud's 24-yard field goal and Podolak's seven-yard touchdown catch from Len Dawson. At 6' 1" and 204 pounds, Podolak was a converted quarterback from Iowa who, in his third pro season, had emerged as rugged and reliable runner. But he had never been this breathtaking. Against Miami he waged one of the most relentless one-man assaults in league history, with 85 yards rushing, 110 yards receiving and 155 yards on returns— or 56% of his team's 623 total yards. Said Dolphins coach Don Shula later, "We still haven't stopped Podolak."

Csonka rumbled across from the one to bring the Dolphins within three points in the second quarter.

112

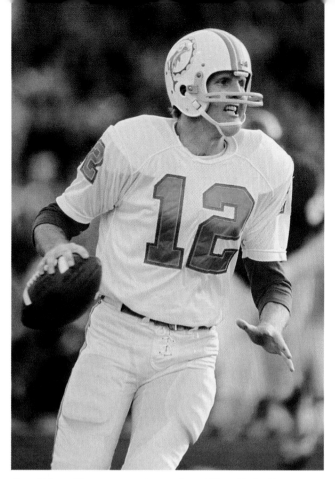

Even Griese, the consummate pro, found himself giggling ...

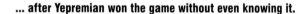

... after Yepremian won the game without even knowing it.

Griese, though, shook off the searing pain in his left shoulder and took on the challenge, tying the score at 10 by halftime. The Chiefs moved ahead 17–10 in the third quarter, but Griese hit six straight passes on a 71-yard drive to draw even by the end of the period. Podolak's second TD edged K.C. ahead 24–17. Griese answered by converting three third downs and completing six of seven throws to four different receivers, the last a five-yarder to tight end Marv Fleming that brought the score to 24 apiece with 1:36 to play.

Enter Yepremian. He kicked off to Podolak, who fielded the ball at the goal line and burst through the first wave of tacklers. Suddenly Podolak was in the clear—except for one cuddly bald man who only twice in his life had attempted a tackle. There were two reasons Yepremian seldom tried. The first was that on one of his attempts, Ray Nitschke had knocked him 15 yards and bloodied his face with a block. In explaining the other reason, Garo showed

his humanitarian streak. "I must protect them from my magnificent body," he said of his opponents.

Yepremian did Podolak no harm, but he did slow him down enough with a shove that Curtis Johnson was able to corral him at the Miami 22. After three running plays, Stenerud trotted onto the field with 35 seconds left for a 32-yard gimme. Despite Yepremian's league-high point total, the established Stenerud had been the AFC's choice for the upcoming Pro Bowl. "Jan just doesn't miss from there," Chiefs coach Hank Stram said afterward.

Jan missed. To the right. By inches. Early in the first overtime Stenerud had another chance to win it, from 42 yards out, but the snap was high and linebacker Nick Buoniconti snuffed the kick. Yepremian subsequently missed from 52 yards, but that failure did not deflate his spirits. "I knew if I had less than 50 yards I would make it," he said.

The mud and the darkness made the coin toss for OT a challenge.

With three minutes gone in the second OT, Miami got possession on its 30 and marched. Csonka blasted 29 yards on "roll right, trap left" called by Griese. It was classic Dolphins stuff, a hint of misdirection followed by a wave of bare-knuckled power, the 237-pound Csonka following the blocks of tackle Norm Evans and guard Larry Little. "I got hold of Larry's pants," Csonka said after the game. "He's faster than I am, and I had to hold on to catch up."

Four plays later, the tie-painter trotted onto the field to break what was shaping up to be an eternal tie. This time, Yepremian's 37-yard kick was good. Unaware that he had put an end to the game and apparently raring for more, he trotted to the sideline to get the kickoff tee.

The game had gone five quarters-plus to sudden death (or sudden victory, as Pollyanna Curt Gowdy insisted on calling it on the TV), from a slug-colored unseasonably warm Missouri afternoon through nightfall. It had been played both crisply and sloppily, with consummate skill and heart-breaking error. It had been dull and heavy, and then exquisitely exciting.

And it went down ultimately to a lightning bolt and a laugh.

At the top what it would seem to have proved beyond the elevation of the Dolphins to the AFC's best bet for the Super Bowl is that Miami's foreign-born place-kicker was better than Kansas City's foreign-born place-kicker, Jan Stenerud of Norway....

**—John Underwood
January 3, 1972**

115

At 7 p.m. on television sets all along the East Coast, the daughter of Julie Andrews and Blake Edwards made her acting debut as a Swiss orphan in braids, yodeling at a herd of mountain goats. Jennifer Edwards was playing the title role in *Heidi*, the fourth flim version of a beloved children's novel, which *The New York Times* had previewed as the best program on TV that day. As a nice man asked Heidi to come live with his sick daughter, some viewers smiled. Others blinked in disbelief. Many picked up their phones and shouted words that would have torched Heidi's braids.

This was no place, and especially no time, for a little girl. Just seconds before, New York had gone up 32–29 in an AFL shootout at Oakland-Alameda County Coliseum on a field littered with fallen bodies and yellow flags. Both teams were 7–2, both were bent on mayhem and both loved to air it out. In anticipation of the surefire AFL action thriller, NBC had cut away from its early game between Buffalo and San Diego at 4 p.m. to show the tilt in its entirety.

The Jets believed that 6'8", 275-pound Raider defensive end Ben Davidson had broken quarterback Joe Namath's cheekbone a year earlier. Just days before the game they learned that there was a photo of Davidson's shot on a wall in Oakland's offices. Asked before the kickoff if the Raiders would be gunning for him, Namath said, "If they want to win, they'd better be."

They were. Oakland sacked him six times. But Namath kept on dropping back and winging away, throwing for 381 yards on 19-of-37 passing. After a fumble by Oakland's Charlie Smith in the fourth quarter, Namath fired for 47 and then 50 yards to wide receiver Don Maynard, who finished with 10 catches for a team-record 228 yards. But

Smith ran for 53 yards against the Jets, including this three-yard plunge for a touchdown in the third quarter.

Heidi's smiling mug (right) kept TV viewers from seeing the game-icing fourth quarter fumble (above).

despite constant reminders from coach Weeb Ewbank, the Jets were unable to keep their poise. They were flagged for a personal foul on the opening kickoff en route to 13 penalties for 145 yards, yet another club record.

Namath's roomie, safety Jim Hudson, flipped out in the third quarter, grabbing a Raiders facemask to draw his second unsportsmanlike conduct penalty and an automatic ejection. This was no game in which to lose a starter in the secondary: Oakland's Daryle (the Mad Bomber) Lamonica was just as nasty as Namath, connecting on 21 of 34 heaves for 311 yards. With a little more than a minute to play, the lead had changed hands five times, and neither team had been up by more than seven. After Davidson was flagged for cheap-shotting Namath, Jim Turner kicked his fourth field goal to snap a 29–all tie with 1:05 to go.

Smith, the Raiders' rookie running back, had just returned Turner's kickoff to the Oakland 22 when the game neared the three-hour mark. NBC cut away to run some ads and give its local affiliates their customary 10 seconds at the top of the hour to identify themselves. In the network's

programming department an executive had a decision to make: stick with football for the last 50 seconds of play or switch to the regularly scheduled, critically acclaimed, sure-to-be-loved-by-children-everywhere show at 7 p.m. For viewers in New York, indeed for anyone east of Denver, that meant one thing: It was Alpine goat time.

When the commercial break ended, apoplectic fans short-circuited the NBC switchboard in New York with protests. Unable to get through, they tied up the police department's emergency lines. They phoned newspapers, the telephone company, the Raiders' office. They hurled popcorn, shoes and invectives at poor, innocent Heidi.

There is, of course, no telling what they might have pelted their sets with had they been able to witness the next 17 seconds of play. After the kickoff Lamonica found Smith for 20 yards; a facemask penalty on Hudson's replacement, Mike D'Amato, moved the ball to New York's 43. On the next play Lamonica picked on D'Amato again, throwing short to Smith, who raced into the end

Namath was sacked six times by Oakland's ferocious defense, but still threw for 381 yards.

zone. With 42 seconds to play, Oakland went ahead 36–32.

Mike Eischeid squibbed his kickoff, bouncing the ball three times before it reached Early Christy at the 15. Christy, duly disrupted, bobbled the ball, then coughed it up under a swarm of Raiders. Preston Ridlchuber, a reserve fullback, picked up the ball and lunged into the Jets' end zone. Over a span of nine pre-empted seconds, Oakland had scored two TDs to defeat New York.

At 8:22, with snow-capped Alps in the background, crawl type informed NBC viewers of the final score. The following morning a *New York Daily News* headline toted up the result this way: JETS 32, OAKLAND 29, 'HEIDI' 14.

SPOTLIGHT

By signing a record $427,000 contract with the New York Jets in 1965, Joe Namath handed the AFL a key victory in its war for parity with the NFL. When he passed for three touchdowns in the Heidi Bowl rematch against Oakland for the 1968 AFL championship, he earned his team a trip to Super Bowl III. And, by making good on his outrageous guarantee of victory over the heavily favored Baltimore Colts, he silenced the hordes of AFL detractors and turned himself into a legend.

Not that he wasn't already a celebrity. From the moment Namath left Alabama for New York, he had the undivided attention of the nation's largest media pool. "He's the biggest thing in New York since Babe Ruth," said Boston Patriot owner Billy Sullivan in 1965. *SI*'s Dan Jenkins labeled him "pro football's very own Beatle." His shaggy hair, good looks, sharp wit and insatiable appetite for life in the fast lane attracted swarms of hangers-on, mostly female. On the field, his famed quick release helped make him the first player to pass for more than 4,000 yards in a single season. Sadly, battered knees forced him to retire at 34 in 1977. Eight years later he was elected to the Hall of Fame.

20/19 GIANTS / BILLS

The field-goal attempt sailed skyward, carrying with it the fate of the two opponents and their diametrically opposed playing styles. For 59 minutes and 52 seconds, the stodgy, smash-mouth Giants and the fluid, fast-breaking Bills had waged a philosophical tug-of-war at Tampa Stadium that made Super Bowl XXV much more compelling than any of its two dozen predecessors. Now the outcome was up in the air and headed toward the uprights as time expired. "The Super Bowl is supposed to come down to the last kick," said Buffalo quarterback Jim Kelly. "If you want to write a script of the game, this is what you have to write."

Kelly was the mastermind of the Bills' no-huddle offense, a rat-a-tat attack designed to keep defenses off-balance and unable to shuttle in new personnel to fit the down and distance. With a veteran line, a pair of gamebreakers in running back Thurman Thomas and wideout Andre Reed and a coolheaded play-caller in Kelly, Buffalo's no-huddle was no-holds-barred. Just two Sundays before, Kelly and Co. had ravaged the Los Angeles Raiders—who had allowed the conference's second-fewest yards during the regular season—by a score of 51–3 in the AFC championship game.

If New York coach Bill Parcells had an antidote to what he deemed Buffalo's "new stuff," it lay in the Lombardian basics he so loved: a bruising running game and a big, bare-knuckle defense that simply, collectively, ground teams into submission. The Giants seldom won on style points—in the NFC title game they beat San Francisco 15–13 on five Matt Bahr field goals—but they never beat themselves. In going 13–3 during the regular season they turned the ball over 14 times, a league-record low. "Yeah, I know we've been called a conservative team," Parcells said before the Super Bowl, "but you'll notice this conservative team is still playing."

As a great game should, Super Bowl XXV came down to the final kick, which drifted just wide of the right upright.

Whether the Super Bowl would be played was uncertain for the 11 days before kickoff. War had broken out in the Persian Gulf, but the game went on. Metal detectors, bomb-sniffing dogs and sharpshooters were deployed at the stadium, and it took each of the 73,813 ticket holders 90 minutes to pass through the gates. Televisions, radios, cameras and umbrellas were banned. In Riyadh, Saudi Arabia, U.S. marines watching the game at 2 a.m. were betting not on its outcome, but on when Saddam Hussein would send the first Scud missile of the night their way.

The Bills were seven-point favorites, in part because they had beaten New York 17–13 on Dec. 15, and knocked out quarterback Phil Simms for the rest of the season with a sprained right arch. After watching the first half of Buffalo's blowout of the Raiders on TV, Parcells gave Giants offensive coordinator Ron Erhardt his marching orders. "Shorten the game," Parcells said.

To keep the ball out of Kelly's hands, Erhardt would depend on a substitute quarterback, Jeff Hostetler, and the oldest starting running back in the league, O.J. Anderson. They were the oddest and most effective offensive couple in Super Bowl history. Hostetler, the first true backup to guide a team to the title, connected on 20 of 32 passes for 222 yards and one TD, time and again turning third downs into firsts. Anderson, age 34, ground out 102 yards on 21 carries and was named the game's MVP. Together they helped the Giants maintain possession for 40:33, more than two-thirds of the game. New York's four scoring marches lasted 11, 10, 14 and 14 plays, respectively.

On defense, the Giants shifted from their customary 3-4 to a 2-3-6 and a 2-4-5 to ensure greater flexibility against the no-huddle and to contain Buffalo's three-wideout sets. While the Bills' no-huddle racked up 218 yards in the first half, it scored only 10 points, with defensive end Bruce Smith

James Lofton and the Bills were hammered relentlessly by Everson Walls and the Giants defense.

sacking Hostetler for a safety to give Buffalo a 12–3 lead, before a TD pass from Hostetler to Stephen Baker late in the second quarter brought the Giants within two. New York's D, meanwhile, was taking its toll. "No other team ever hit me this hard," Reed said. "You can't even compare this to anything I've ever been through. They bruised up my whole body."

Anderson barreled in from the one to put the Giants up 17–12 in the third quarter.

The Giants regained the lead, 17–12, with the only score of the third quarter, a one-yard TD run by Anderson. Buffalo responded in the fourth with a 31-yard dash by Thomas, who was indomitable (15 carries for 135 yards, five catches for 55 more). Back came New York with a 21-yard Bahr field goal that made it 20–19 . Taking over on his own 10-yard line with 2:16 to go, Kelly gobbled up 51 yards in 2:08. Scott Norwood trotted out to try to win the Super Bowl with a 47-yard field goal, one yard less than his longest conversion of the year.

On the New York sideline a kneeling Hostetler looked away, toward the stands, "watching the people," he would say. "Capturing the moment." Adam Lingner snapped the ball. Frank Reich spotted it. Norwood kicked it strong and straight and toward the right upright—until it tailed off. The kick drifted two feet wide of the post.

The Giants had won their second Super Bowl in five years by the slimmest possible margin. "We played as well as we could," Parcells said. "If we played tomorrow, Buffalo would probably win."

"Power wins football games," Parcells repeated endlessly amidst the postgame locker room turmoil. "Power wins football games."

That philosophy has permeated his approach to the game: Draft big, powerful people to play on both sides of the ball, grind out a rushing game behind a hog-type line ... stuff the run on defense and, when the other team passes, make sure the routes are short and the receivers are funneled to the linebackers. Big people attacking little people. It's a rather brutal concept, and on Sunday, it resulted in a whopping advantage in possession

In SI's Words

time—40:33 to 19:27—that left the Bills' defenders groggy and rubber-legged....

The Parcells approach is an answer to the new trends, the blue plate specials of 1990, like the run-and-shoot and Buffalo's three-wideout, no-huddle offense. It's a rather quaint reversion to the days before sock 'em gave way to slick 'em. Someone asked Parcells if Super Bowl XXV had vindicated his system. "It's always been vindicated," he said. "It's the new stuff that had something to prove."

—Paul Zimmerman
February 4, 1991

LIONS / BROWNS

December 27, 1953

With Bobby Layne in command, the Detroit huddle was a swirl of whiskey fumes, X-rated humor and boundless promise. Layne was a 27-year-old from Santa Anna, Texas, as spirited as a stallion and as predictable as a tumbleweed. Whether he was tossing around $100 bills at a showbar on Saturday night or selling out his 6' 1", 201-pound body on Sunday afternoon, he thrived on leading by indomitable example. The Lions knew there was no gambit Layne wouldn't try—and couldn't pull off—with money on the line.

There were slightly more than two minutes left in the NFL Championship Game when Layne took timeout and sidled over to talk with coach Buddy Parker. Detroit trailed visiting Cleveland 16–10 at Briggs Stadium, and stood 33 yards away from the go-ahead touchdown and a second straight title. Parker, noting the Browns hard pass rush, suggested a screen pass to Layne. "Know what I think?" Layne told Parker. "I think a cigarette sure would taste good about now."

Normally, Layne could have afforded such diversions when facing the Browns. Cleveland coach Paul Brown's team had never beaten Parker's, and on this day Cleveland quarterback Otto Graham was practically delivering Detroit the crown with his badly chapped hands. After connecting on 64.8% of his passes during the regular season, Graham had completed just two of 15 throws for 20 yards and committed two costly turnovers. In the first quarter he fumbled to set up Doak Walker's one-yard TD run over left tackle, and in the second, Jim David picked off Graham, which led to a Walker field goal.

But the Lions weren't distinguishing themselves on the soft and slippery turf either. End Leon Hart injured a knee

Layne's extracurricular carousing never prevented him from getting the job done on the field.

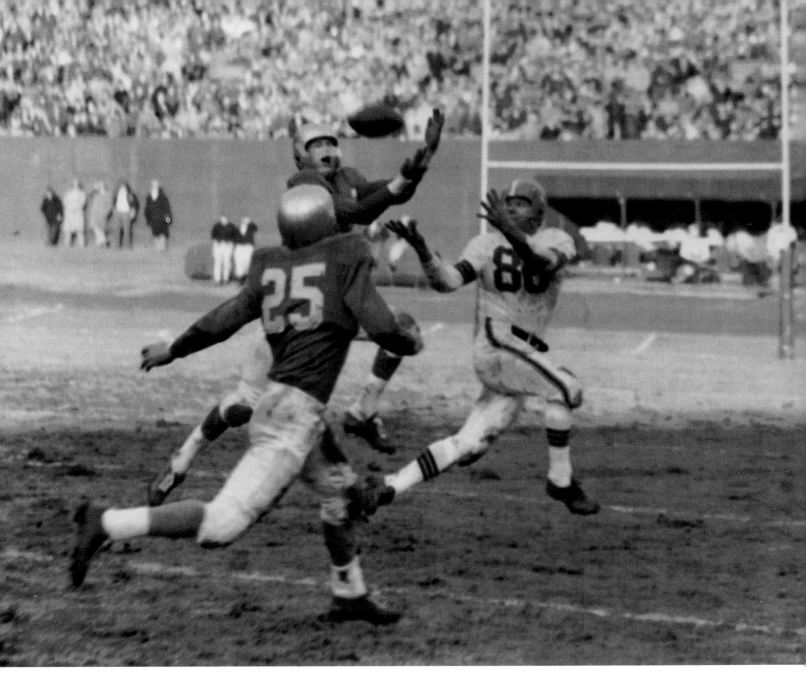

Graham was uncharacteristically ineffective, throwing two interceptions, including this one by Detroit DB Jack Christiansen.

soon after the opening kickoff, Walker botched two field goals and Detroit's most inspired play was called back. After David's interception and return to the Cleveland 20, Layne pitched to Walker, his former teammate at Highland Park (Texas) High. He flipped a short pass to Layne, who snaked in for what appeared to be a touchdown. But as the ball was spotted for the extra point, Cleveland cornerback Warren Lahr persuaded the refs to nullify the score. Because Layne had received a hand-to-hand snap from the center, he was—according to Rule 7, Section 5, Article 2, Item 1, Notice D—ineligible. The Lions had to settle for Walker's 22-yard kick, which put them up 10–3.

Chick Jagade's nine-yard touchdown run in the third quarter and two Lou Groza field goals in the fourth sent the Browns out in front 16–10. With 4:10 remaining Layne took over on his own 20. "Y'all block," he told the offense, "and ol' Bobby'll pass you right to the championship."

With Hart sidelined, ol' Bobby would have to make due with Hart's backup, Jim Doran. A gentleman farmer from Boone, Iowa, in his third year with the Lions, Doran had caught six balls during the season, none for touchdowns. But he kept telling Layne in the huddle that he could beat Lahr, and Layne was inclined to agree. "Jimmy Doran had good hands," Layne said. "And he wasn't the type to go off saying things if he wasn't pretty damn sure."

On the first snap Layne drilled a 17-yarder to Doran. On third-and-10 he found Doran again, this time on a lunging grab between two defenders for 18 yards. Three plays later Detroit was on the Cleveland 33, and Parker was stumping for the screen. Layne, as usual, went his own way, and called Nine Up. "Just throw it," Doran said. "I'll beat him."

Lahr lined up in tight coverage on the right side, and Doran came out as if to block, his forearm raised. Lahr bit on the fake and Doran blew by him to the roar of the 54,577 fans in the stands. "I raced toward the end zone and looked up," he said, "and there was the ball."

NFL commissioner Bert Bell had advised the teams that they would play "sudden death" if the game was tied at the end of regulation. But Walker, with Layne holding, banged in the extra point, and with 2:08 to play, Detroit held a one-point lead. Cleveland's comeback attempt lasted all of one play, when Graham threw an interception to rookie defensive back Carl Karilivacz. Afterward, Brown couldn't bring himself to talk directly about Layne's brilliance or Graham's stunning ineptitude. "It was the toughest game we've ever lost," he said. "I doubt if any team ever lost a tougher one."

Doran grabbed this 18-yard pass to keep the winning drive alive.

The Cleveland Browns were in the midst of one of the greatest—and most unrecognized—runs in pro football history when they met the Lions for the 1953 NFL championship. Having won four straight titles in a rival league, the All-America Football Conference (AAFC), Cleveland joined the NFL in 1950 and reached the championship game in each of its first six seasons, winning three titles. But the Detroit Lions shadowed the Browns throughout, reeling off three straight title appearances of their own during the Cleveland reign. The

AFTERMATH

'53 nail-biter was the second straight victory by the Lions over the Browns in the NFL title game, and both were bitter pills for Cleveland to swallow. In '52 the Browns picked up 22 first downs to the Lions' 10, but lost, 17–7, thanks to the Motor City D, which repeatedly stiffened in its own territory. The Browns would have their revenge in '54, routing Detroit 56–10. After the historic Cleveland run ended in '55, the two teams attached a coda to their rivalry, meeting for the NFL championship in '57. Detroit, led by Tobin Rote, got the last word, winning 59–14.

FANTASTIC FINISHES

The wing was Staubach's (left), and his winning pass the prayer; Roman Gabriel (above) and the Rams needed a blocked punt to produce their miracle finish.

OVERVIEW

The first 59 minutes are a delicious prelude; the magic happens in the final one. The ebb and flow of a high-stakes game become distilled into 60 seconds in which the verdict is in doubt and a sensational play— or a series of them—is the ultimate difference. Sometimes these endings are so grand they are assigned names with capital letters that become woven into the game's folklore. Here are the grandest ones.

The Immaculate Reception. Like the Immaculate Conception, this moment is ripe with mystery. Did Steelers running back Frenchy Fuqua, the self-styled count, touch the ball that deflected off Oakland Raiders safety Jack Tatum and into the hands of Pittsburgh running back Franco Harris? If Fuqua did touch it, the pass should have been ruled incomplete. As it was, Harris's catch propelled Pittsburgh to a 13–7 victory in the 1972 AFC playoffs. Replays were inconclusive and, a quarter of a century later, Fuqua hadn't divulged his side of the story.

The Catch. Skeptics have long wondered whether the play was a fluke. Surely San Francisco 49ers quarterback Joe Montana could only have been desperately guessing when he zinged that pass toward Dwight Clark, who reached for the ball and caught the stars. In that single, outsized moment in the 1982 NFC championship game, the Niners shook off the jinx that the Dallas Cowboys had placed on them and advanced to the first of their five Super Bowls—all victories.

Hail Mary. The wing belonged to Cowboys quarterback Roger Staubach. The prayer was the high spiral he heaved toward Drew Pearson in the 1975 NFC playoff game against the Minnesota Vikings. In this case there was no doubt about the flukiness of the

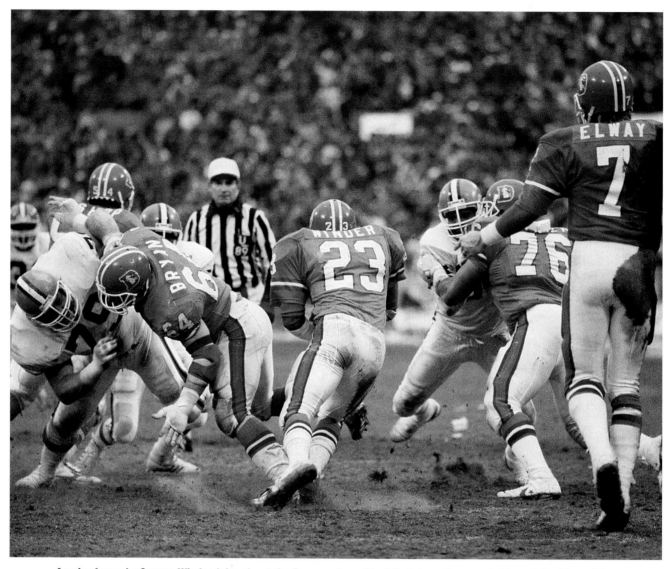

A pair of runs by Sammy Winder (above) got the Broncos the critical first down they needed to get the Elway drive started, while the Montana drive included three passes to running back Roger Craig (right) for 29 yards.

touchdown pass: It was a one-in-a-hundred shot slung from 50 yards away for the victory.

The Drive. The Montana era began with The Catch; it ended with The Drive. Down 16–13 to the Cincinnati Bengals in Super Bowl XXIII, Montana completed eight of nine throws to march 92 yards for the winning TD in the final 3:10. For Joe Cool, that near-flawless display under pressure earned him Super Bowl ring No. III.

The Drive. Though this is the same moniker applied to Montana's heroics, to certain sets of fans it can only mean another last-gasp advance: the Denver Broncos' in '87. Many of those fans reside in Cleveland, where the 98½-yard charge is remembered with nearly unbearable pain. By going the distance, quarterback John Elway cancelled the Browns' trip to Pasadena for what would have been their first Super Bowl.

Perhaps because it didn't happen in the postseason, the Los Angeles Rams' game-winning play against the Green Bay Packers in 1967 has never been summed up in a couple of words. We'll call it *The Block*—it belongs.

Pittsburgh quarterback Terry Bradshaw had thrown three straight incompletions and now, with 22 seconds left to play in Pittsburgh's first postseason apearance in a quarter-century, he was faced with fourth down on his own 40-yard line. Just 51 seconds earlier Oakland backup quarterback Kenny (The Snake) Stabler had finally pierced the Steel Curtain defense on a 30-yard TD scramble. The Raiders led 7–6 in the AFC playoff semifinal. Sizing up the moment later, Oakland coach John Madden would say, "There is no tomorrow. You're down to a fourth-down play. One play. You play twenty-one ballgames for this moment—fourth down."

The 50,350 fans jammed into Three Rivers Stadium watched, their hearts in their hardhats. Members of the kitschy fan clubs that had arisen to revel in the franchise's revival—Gerela's Gorillas, Franco's Italian Army, Fuqua's Foreign Legion—crossed their fingers. Long-suffering Steelers owner Art Rooney, extinguishing his ever-present cigar, made his way to the elevator. He wanted to reach the locker room early so that he could make a few private remarks to his valiant, vanquished team. But if such moments of despair have a virtue, it is this: Only in them can a miracle take place.

In the Steelers' huddle Bradshaw barked out, "66 Option." One more completion, he hoped, would put kicker Roy Gerela in position to send his fan club into a simian frenzy with his third field goal of the game. Across the line, Raiders safety Jack Tatum glowered, muttering, "One more time, one more time, one more time."

Bradshaw took the snap from center Mike Webster and dropped back seven steps, searching for an open man. To his right, defensive linemen Otis Sistrunk and Tony Cline

Harris's 42-yard dash to the end zone capped one of the most bizarre—and controversial—finishes in NFL history.

Bradshaw, who ended up flat on his back, had to wait for the replays to see the miraculous catch by Harris.

crashed into the Pittsburgh backfield. As Bradshaw drifted right to avoid the rush, rookie fullback Franco Harris, who was supposed to stay in and pass-protect, instinctively headed downfield, where he could give the embattled Bradshaw an outlet target. "But then," Harris said, "Terry threw it deep."

At the Raiders' 35-yard line, Harris's running mate, Frenchy Fuqua, hooked and braced for Bradshaw's bul-

let. A self-proclaimed count reincarnate whose rococo wardrobe included clear platform shoes with goldfish swimming in the heels, Fuqua loved to play the flake off the field. On it, though, he was a starch fundamentalist, and in anticipation of Tatum's closing in from behind, he made sure to place himself between the defender and the ball. Tatum, a sniper in the backfield, had struck so much fear in receivers that he could have created a new position: the un-safety.

Both ball and Raider reached Fuqua at the same moment, Tatum's blow conjuring up images of a runaway truck. "I thought I had the ball," Fuqua recalled, "and just then I had the accident."

As the ball ricocheted seven yards upfield, a prone Bradshaw flung his helmet in disgust. Not until he saw the TV replays did Bradshaw witness the work of the Steelers' thaumaturge: Harris. Franco's explanation later—"Reaction moves your hands"—conveyed the unflappable way in which he had swooped in on the wobbly ball, snatched it with his fingertips at the last possible instant before it touched the Astroturf, and sprinted 42 yards past the stunned Raiders into the end zone. Still descending in the elevator, Rooney could only hear the crowd roar at this divine event: the Immaculate Reception.

As hundreds of fans poured onto the field, Tatum railed at a jubilant Fuqua. "Tell them you touched it! Tell them you touched it!" he shouted. Until 1978, the NFL's rules prevented an offensive player from deflecting a ball to his teammate. Madden claimed the pass was incomplete because it had touched not Tatum, but two Steelers consecutively. In what some believe was the league's first use of replay to determine a contested call, Art McNally, the league's senior official in the press box, spoke with referee Fred Swearingen on the field-level telephone. As reported by the *Los Angeles Times*, the conversation went as follows:

"What are you going to call that play, Fred?" McNally asked.

"I'm going to call it a touchdown. It was a legal catch."

Officials were clearly right in ruling Harris's catch (above) legal, but what about the questionable deflection?

"That's correct," McNally said.

Later, after the game's final five seconds were played, Madden tried to make sense of what had happened. "The ball bounces off one man's chest into another man's arms, and it's over," he said. "No tomorrow. I'm telling you this will hurt for a long, long time."

It takes time to erect a "steel curtain" from the bottom of a rubble heap strewn with decades of ridicule and losing records. And although Pittsburgh lost 21–17 in the AFC championship game to Miami in 1972, and was stopped the following year in the division playoffs in a rematch against Oakland (33–14), the core of the team that would go on to win an unprecedented four Super Bowls in a decade had been forged.

AFTERMATH

No fewer than five future Hall of Famers were on the Immaculate Reception roster: Terry Bradshaw, whose regular season stats might not measure up against other Hall of Fame quarterbacks, was peerless in the playoffs. Franco Harris, who as a rookie headlined in what is perhaps the most frequently run highlight clip in NFL history, became the league's alltime Super Bowl rushing leader. The biggest star, though, was Pittsburgh's now famous "Steel Curtain" defense—led by defensive tackle "Mean" Joe Greene, cornerback Mel Blount and linebacker Jack Ham. The Curtain came crashing down on Minnesota's Super Bowl title hopes in 1975. It did the same to Dallas in '76 and '79, and again to Los Angeles in '80.

Before the game-winning throw, Montana was less than stellar.

Dwight Clark's leaping, laid-out, last-gasp fingertip grab in the back corner of Candlestick Park's north end zone that defeated Dallas in the NFC Championship Game has been reduced to a pair of words: The Catch. Clark's amazing handiwork etched one moment so deeply in the minds of Bay Area residents that they mark events by it (e.g., "It was at the party the night before The Catch"). Unfortunately, constant use of The Catch phrase has minimized all

the drama that went before and after it. Here are some other summations:

•The Stakes. In Bill Walsh's first season as the 49ers' coach they went 2–14. Two years later they were an NFL-best 13–3. The Cowboys, however, were a test San Francisco had forever failed. In three straight seasons, from 1970 to '72, Dallas had knocked the Niners out of the playoffs, twice in the NFC title game. "There was some arrogance about being a Cowboy," Clark said. "They came in like they were the established team looking to kick the young upstarts' butts."

•The Preamble. Over the first 55 minutes, San Francisco seized the lead three times (7–0, 14–10, 21–17); Dallas snatched it back three times (10–7, 17–14, 27–21). A crowd of 60,525, the largest in Candlestick history, pounded its collective forehead in frustration and dismay. The home team would roll up 393 yards and a season-high 26 first downs while holding the Cowboys to 250 yards, 117.5 below their season average. But the 49ers committed six turnovers, including three interceptions thrown by their third-year quar-

In an apt description, Dallas defensive back Everson Walls said Clark "played a little over his head" on his dramatic grab.

138

The victory yielded a pair of firsts for the jubilant 49er fans: a first NFC title and a first trip to the Super Bowl.

terback out of Notre Dame, Joe Montana. The Niners had a shot at hoisting their first trophy in franchise history, and they were handling it like wet soap. "Montana has to be the key," Cowboy coach Tom Landry said. "There's nothing else there except him."

•The Drive. With 4:54 to play, the 25-year-old Montana took over on his own 11-yard line, down six. "I was very confident in the huddle," he said after the game. "We had to move the ball, and we knew we could." Walsh and offensive coordinator Sam Wyche reflected that assuredness in their play calling. Rather than rush straight to the air, they threw a medley of runs—sweeps right and left, a trap and a reverse—at a Dallas prevent defense larded with six defensive backs. Instead of trying to eat up the yardage they took reasonable bites: No play advanced more than 14 yards.

With Montana completing five of seven passes for 39

yards, the 49ers briskly moved to the Dallas six in 12 plays. Facing third-and-three with 58 seconds to go, San Francisco called timeout. Walsh called for Montana to roll right and throw to Freddie Solomon across the middle or high to the 6'4" Clark. On fourth down, Lenvil Elliott would sweep left.

•The Throw. Sprint Right Option was one of the first plays Walsh put in at summer training camp in Rocklin. Montana and Clark, best friends and roommates, hated it. "It wasn't an easy route for Dwight," Montana said. "And at practice it was hard to throw while running and jumping. [Walsh] would say, 'No, No. Throw it harder, throw it higher.' "

Walsh didn't like to tip his hand by varying his sets or using the shotgun; he had both backs in, with Clark and Solomon split right. Montana took the snap and rolled out, but Dallas blitzed and the pass rush of D.D. Lewis and Ed (Too Tall) Jones and Larry Bethea forced him to accelerate toward the sideline. Too Tall was too close, cutting off Montana's chance of finding Solomon in the middle. "I couldn't see anyone except Jones," Montana said afterward. Sensing the out-of-bounds line near, Montana threw off his back foot to where he thought Clark was. As hard and as high as he could.

•The Victim. To this point 6'1" rookie Dallas cornerback Everson Walls had been the star of the game. He had made a key fumble recovery, two interceptions and eight tackles. Walls was assigned to Clark, but Solomon, sliding across the middle, had screened him slightly. Still, Walls had good position as Montana fired and fell back. When he saw the ball zipping toward the grandstand, he did not leave his feet. "To me, it looked way up there," Walls said. "I misjudged where it was going. I think Clark played a little over his head on that catch. He had to jump higher than he ever did before."

•The Fumble. Ray Wersching's extra point gave the Niners the lead, but the Cowboys weren't finished. With a 31-yard pass from Danny White to Drew Pearson—only a neck tackle by cornerback Eric Wright prevented Pearson from scoring—Dallas was on the Niners' 46, a modest gain away from field goal range and possible victory. On the next play, Lawrence Pillers blasted through the Dallas line and forced White to cough up the ball. End Jim Stuckey recovered. San Francisco would make its first trip to the Super Bowl.

An hour later Stuckey, fully dressed, walked through the Niners locker room. He had a toothbrush in one hand and that ball in the other.

A 26-yard White-to-Tony Hill strike staked Dallas to a 10–7 lead.

The reverse gained 14 yards to the Cowboy 35, then Montana drilled Split End Dwight Clark on an out pattern, right, for 10 more, a very risky, low-percentage pass into the teeth of double coverage by Everson Walls, who'd already intercepted two, and Nickel Back Benny Barnes. "Walls actually got a hand on it," Clark said. "Then the ball hit me in the chest." "I thought it would be a knockdown for Walls," Montana said.

A minute and a half left now. Montana hit Solomon on an underneath pattern for 12, down to the 13-yard line, and the 49ers called time

In SI's Words

with 1:15 showing. Clark slowly sank to the ground. Hal Wyatt, the co-trainer, went out to him. "You O.K.?" he asked. "Water, gimme some water," Clark said. Half a dozen

Cowboys were on one knee, heads down, chests heaving. "I looked over at them," [Randy] Cross said. "They had, well, I don't want to say, a beaten look, but I saw on their faces the same look Thomas Hearns had when Sugar Ray hit him a few times. They had had us backed up, but now they were no longer the aggressors. They were fighting for their lives."
—Paul Zimmerman
January 18, 1982

A small, bright object whizzed past Dallas wideout Drew Pearson near the Minnesota goal line, and only one thought crossed his mind: penalty flag. He had just caught a wobbly pass that had covered 50 yards of cold, gray sky, a desperation heave that struck Pearson in the crotch before he tucked it against his right hip with his elbow and then gathered it into his hands. Now, as he negotiated the last few yards before paydirt with the winning touchdown, Pearson was sure that his grab would be called back.

Until this drive Pearson, who had made 46 receptions during the regular season, had not caught a pass in the NFC first-round playoff game against the heavily favored Vikings—hadn't even had one thrown his way. "Drew was getting mad at me because he said he'd been getting open and I wasn't finding him," quarterback Roger Staubach said. With 44 seconds to go Dallas was mired on its own 25-yard line, trailing 14–10. Pearson ran a 25-yard corner pattern in front of Nate Wright, one of the cornerbacks who had muzzled him. Wright shoved him as he made the catch, so even though both of Pearson's feet weren't in bounds, the officials ruled it a reception at midfield.

The crowd at Metropolitan Stadium, eager to see their 12–2 Vikings return to the Super Bowl, groaned and fidgeted. "I can beat Wright deep," Pearson told Staubach in the huddle, "but give me a chance to catch my breath."

Staubach did, tossing an incompletion over the middle. Then he said the words Pearson wanted to hear: streak route. Dallas coach Tom Landry credited Staubach with calling the play. "I was just standing on the sideline feeling very disappointed we had played so well and were going to lose," Landry said. "I knew our only chance was to throw one long and hope for a miracle."

Staubach, a master of the last-minute comeback, engineered yet another one with his miraculous heave to Pearson.

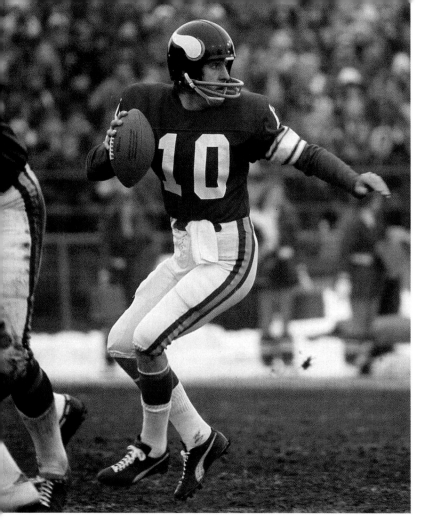

Tarkenton later learned of his father's fatal heart attack.

Pearson, split right, set off down the sideline. He made a small feint to the middle about 15 yards downfield, then switched into high gear. Wright turned to catch up and Staubach felt a momentary surge of hope. "When a defender takes his eyes off the ball," he said, "strange things can happen." Staubach let fly as far as his badly bruised ribs

would allow. His heave hung a little, and Pearson slowed at the five-yard line to get a bead on the ball. As he did, Wright went in front of him, and the two jostled for position like power forwards boxing out for a rebound. Then Wright fell. He had slipped. Or tripped. Or been pushed.

Pearson waltzed into the end zone as Wright lay flat on his back, resulting in what one writer would call, "the most enormous swell of silence in the history of gatherings of 46,425 wearers of the purple." While watching that play unfold, however, one fan had refused to take the moment with complete resignation, hurling an orange onto the field. That small, bright, whizzing object—not a penalty flag for pass interference—had slowed Pearson's progress. The TD stood.

Seconds later another fan registered his disapproval, throwing a large glass object at Armen Terzian, the field judge. The pint of whiskey knocked him down and left a V-shaped gash in the middle of his forehead.

The non-call was not the first controversy of the game. On a second-quarter punt the refs ruled that Dallas return man Cliff Harris had touched the ball, even though replays revealed that he hadn't. Minnesota recovered at the four-yard line and soon took a 7–0 lead. Behind Staubach the Cowboys, a wild-card playoff entry, came back to lead 10–7 early in the fourth quarter on Toni Fritsch's 24-yard field goal. But quarterback Fran Tarkenton and running back Chuck Foreman, bottled up all day by the Dallas Doomsday Defense, steered the Vikings on an 11-play, 70-yard TD drive to reclaim the lead with 5:11 to go.

Tarkenton's dad, the Reverend Dallas Tarkenton, was watching the game at his home in Savannah, Ga. During

In SI's Words

Usually it only happens in those novels written for young readers. It is cold and gloomy and all hope seems to be gone, but the good guy who loves his wife and family and country has gone back to try one more long pass against the evil villains who throw bottles and garbage at football officials. The ball sails high and far, 50 yards into the frozen atmosphere, a silly object, it seems, straining to be seen against the feeble lights that glow through the gray Minnesota sky. Now the ball is coming to earth as the scoreboard flickers away the final seconds of the game. There are two men underneath the ball and suddenly one of them slips and falls, and the one who is supposed to catch it and complete the grandest of comebacks and upsets and fairy tales does exactly that. Roger Staubach has thrown a pass to Drew Pearson and the Dallas Cowboys have used up a lifetime of good fortune in a single play to stun the Minnesota Vikings and grasp a victory they had richly deserved all day long.
—Dan Jenkins
January 5, 1976

the commercial break after the Viking's go-ahead score, he suffered a fatal heart attack. Tarkenton would learn shortly after the game that his 63-year-old father had died.

The Cowboys' last drive began at their own 15-yard line with 1:51 left. It ended on what Staubach called a Hail Mary pass. "You throw it up," he said, "and pray."

After the game, neither Pearson nor Wright could confidently reconstruct the play. "I might've put my hands on him, but I don't think I pushed off," said Pearson. "I really can't say for sure," Wright allowed.

On the Minnesota sideline, however, there was little hedging. "It was as clear as night and day that Nate was pushed," Minnesota coach Bud Grant said. "A receiver will get away with that once in a hundred times. If he's caught, the ball simply goes back and they try it again. It's the old basketball play. You simply push off and jump up for the ball." Wherever the truth lay, Pearson had snatched a brown, oblong wobbling object and taken it into the end zone. And with it he grabbed an upset victory.

Pearson's game-winning catch was the answer to Staubach's fervent prayer of a pass.

Most of the 49ers were hyperventilating after their fourth-quarter, 82-yard double-time march on a steamy Miami night with Super Bowl XXIII in the balance. San Francisco trailed 16–13 and had just reached the Cincinnati 10-yard line. San Francisco had taken a timeout, the second one spent during the drive. In the Niner huddle chests heaved as quarterback Joe Montana assessed the lay of the land. "Hey, look over there," he said to his linemen, gesturing to the stands. "There's John Candy."

The sight of Uncle Buck's alter ego among 75,159 fans was truly more distracting to Montana than his team's dire straits. From the 1979 Cotton Bowl, when he led Notre Dame past Houston, to the '82 NFC title game defeat of the Cowboys to Super Bowl XVI, also against the Bengals, Montana had demonstrated an Einstein-like facility for solving problems of time (limited) and space (much). Was another do-or-die drive at hand? Ball on the 49ers' eight-yard line, 3:10 to play, three timeouts left, three points down. Call two plays at a time, manage the clock, chew up yardage in chunks and avoid the one mistake that can unravel an entire season's work? Fine. Let's see. . . who else can we find in the crowd? Eugene Levy?

As San Francisco took over, a Bengal teammate told wide receiver Cris Collinsworth on the sidelines, "We got them now." Recalled Collinsworth, "I said, 'Have you taken a look at who's quarterbacking the San Francisco 49ers?' That's what it came down to. Joe Montana is not human. I don't want to call him a god, but he's definitely somewhere in between."

The numbers qualify Montana for apotheosis. The 49ers Super Bowl–winning drive covered 102 yards because of a holding penalty. Montana picked up 97 of them in 2:36.

As he had done so many times in the past, Montana remained Joe Cool in the pocket and under pressure.

147

Taylor celebrated the game-winning touchdown in high style.

nary Joe. He had completed 15 of 27 passes for 260 yards, and hadn't steered the Niners into the end zone until one minute into the fourth quarter, when he whistled a 14-yard pass to wide receiver Jerry Rice. That tied the game at 13. Cincinnati's Boomer Esiason responded with a 10-play march that ended with Jim Breech's 40-yard field goal. Only a year earlier the Bengals had finished 4–11. Now they were on the verge of winning their first NFL championship and denying the 49ers their third.

The preceding hours had gone none too smoothly for the Bengals. The team's hotel, the Omni International, was only six blocks from Overtown, a predominantly black neighborhood that had been the site of weeklong rioting after a policeman shot and killed a speeding black motorist. From their hotel rooms the Bengals could see fires blazing nearby. After missing the team's 8 p.m. meeting the night before the game, fullback Stanley Wilson was found high on cocaine in his hotel room, and the NFL immediately suspended him for violating the league's substance-abuse policy. On the first play of their second possession, All-Pro noseguard Tim Krumrie, the anchor of the Cincinnati defense, shattered two bones in his left leg.

The turf had also claimed 49ers offensive tackle Steve Wallace, who broke his left ankle on the first series of the game. The grounds crew had forgotten to turn off the suction system the night before, leaving the field so dry that patches of sod came up on every play. That kept two normally well-fueled attacks down: Fans waited a Super Bowl–record 44:26 of play for the first TD, and that came on a 93-yard kickoff return by the Bengals' Stanford Jennings.

He threw nine passes and completed eight, none for more than 27 yards, most right down the middle, the last a 10-yard strike to split end John Taylor. He never raised his voice, never lost his cool. "In the huddle guys were saying, 'I can do it,' and we were telling them, 'Not *can* do it. You're *gonna* do it,' " center Randy Cross said after the game. "And we did it. Anybody who thought Joe Montana had a peer might reconsider that now."

Before the last drive began, Montana had been an ordi-

Rice, playing on a swollen right ankle, had to adjust to the conditions, and he did. Instead of running multiple-cut patterns he relied on fades, diagonals, quick ins or outs and the occasional streak. He caught 11 passes for a Super Bowl–record 215 yards and was named the game's MVP. "Jerry's like a Mike Tyson, a Michael Jordan, a Joe Montana," said former 49ers receiver Dwight Clark, "He's a step above the field."

No one needed Montana's touchdown signal to recognize that he had manufactured yet another miracle finish.

Rice's final catch was the key to the winning drive. On second-and-20 from Cincinnati's 45 he snagged a square-in 13 yards downfield, then knifed through the secondary for 14 more yards. "It had to be a perfect throw and catch," said Bengals cornerback Lewis Billups. "He had all kinds of hands flashing in front of him."

Two plays later Montana called 20 Halfback Curl X-Up and hit his secondary receiver, Taylor, in the end zone. Joe Cool had salvaged another improbable victory.

"We were only 34 seconds away," said Bengals coach Sam Wyche. "Just 34."

The Niners had the ball on Cincy's 23, and again they came up a yard short of a crucial first down, but Mike Cofer's 32-yard field goal made the score 6–6 with 0:50 remaining in the third quarter. It looked as if a Super Bowl would be tied going into the fourth quarter for the first time ever.

But Stanford Jennings, whose wife had had a baby girl the night before

In SI's Words

and who had dreamed of running a kick back all the way as a kind of present for little Kelsey, did just that with the ensuing kickoff. He went 93 yards down the middle of the field without breaking stride or making a cut. The wedge in front of Jennings—tackles

David Douglas and Jim Rourke, line-backers Leon White and Leo Barker—had swept the board clean.

The Bengals led 13–6, and still no touchdowns had been scored by either offensive unit. All of a sudden the game opened up, and the Super Bowl everyone will remember began.

—Paul Zimmerman
January 30, 1989

27 / 24
RAMS / PACKERS

The Rams needed wins in their final two games to reach the playoffs, and they weren't getting one of them. All of quarterback Roman Gabriel's heroics and coach George Allen's exhortations and the L.A. defense's fortitude were 55 seconds from meaninglessness as Donny Anderson of the Packers faded back to punt at the Los Angeles Coliseum. The Packers led 24–20; the Rams had no timeouts remaining. Tickets to L.A.'s season finale "were being devalued faster than the British pound," wrote *Los Angeles Times* columnist Jim Murray.

What Allen called his "special unit forces"—the special teams—had done little to conjure up much hope for the home crowd of 76,637. The Packers' first touchdown, a 30-yard pass from Bart Starr to Carroll Dale, had come four plays after Lee Roy Caffey swatted Bruce Gossett's 46-yard field goal attempt, a maneuver that delighted Packers coach Vince Lombardi. "The game will become sophisticated beyond my wildest dreams," he said. "But desire will always be the larger part of football. To block a kick requires the maximum effort and desire."

Said a Rams official, "Looks like the same old story. The Packers wait until we make a mistake—and wham."

But Los Angeles had discovered more fight under Allen, who took over in 1966 and one year later had the Rams 9-1-2 and in the hunt for the Coastal Division title. The L.A. D held Starr and Co. to just three plays in a 13-minute stretch, while Gabriel dialed up wide receiver Jack Snow for a pair of touchdowns. The Rams led 17–10 late in the third quarter.

Just when the Rams' defense and offense were clicking, however, the special unit arrived. For the most part, Gossett had squibbed his kickoffs out of respect for Travis (the

Guillory (88) burst through unscathed to block Anderson's punt and set up the game-winning score two plays later.

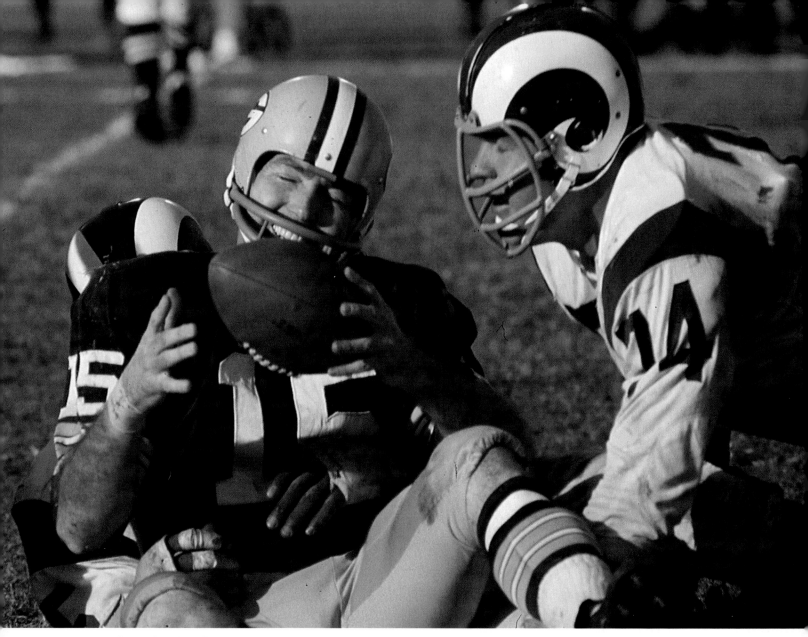

In spite of directing what seemed to be a game-winning 57-yard scoring drive, Starr for once did not get the last laugh.

Roadrunner) Williams, effectively bottling him up. At 6'1" and 210 pounds with legit 9.3 speed in the 100, Williams already had returned three kicks for TDs in '67, tying an NFL record. This time Gossett's boot traveled four yards past the Green Bay goal line. "We like to change our tactics on the kickoffs according to the situation," Allen said. "Anyway, we thought we could contain him."

The Roadrunner exploded that strategy like a package from the Acme Company. He blasted out of the end zone and crashed into tackle Bob Nichols at the 15-yard line. While the collision knocked Nichols out of one shoe, Williams bounced three yards sideways and roared toward the sideline to go the 104-yard distance. The game was tied.

Once again, L.A. refused to fold. Cornerback Clancy Williams's interception set up a Gossett field goal that made it 20–17 Rams. But after a defensive stop, Rams running back Dick Bass fumbled, and Starr directed a go-ahead, 57-yard TD drive to put the Packers in front 24–20. When L.A. failed to convert on a fourth down, Green Bay took over on its 44. Three runs for minus-three yards and three timeouts later, the left-footed Anderson prepared to take the deep snap from Ken Bowman. Many headed for their cars to beat the traffic. Lombardi's Packers had once again proved to be too poised, too much.

The Rams had worked on their punt-blocking techniques at least once a week in practice. Special teams coach Marion Campbell deployed nine men on the line of scrimmage, rather than his usual seven. Some of them even the team's paymaster would be hard-pressed to identify. Flanked to one side was reserve defensive back Claude Crabb; substitute linebacker Tony Guillory lined up directly over Bowman. Both poured through the line, and up-back Tommy Joe Crutcher quickly moved to cut off Crabb. Guillory, surprised to come through clean, roared at Anderson.

The next sound was one Anderson had never heard: the dull thud of his punt being blocked. Lunging with Lombardian effort and desire, his arms outstretched and crossed, Guillory snuffed it with his left wrist. The ball wobbled toward Crabb, who picked it up and sped toward the end zone surrounded by a herd of Rams—including Guillory, who nearly tripped him up. "I can't see without my glasses," he explained. "I didn't know Claude had the ball, and I couldn't read the numbers anyway."

Somehow Anderson weaved in and tackled Crabb at the Packers' five. L.A. had 44 seconds left to score. After an incompletion the Rams lined up in a tight, running formation with end Bernie Casey just outside left tackle. Gabriel faked a handoff to Tommy Mason, and Casey came out as if to block cornerback Bob Jeter. When Jeter bought the run, Casey slipped into the corner of the end zone and hauled in Gabriel's feathery toss for the deciding score.

But not the deciding play. That belonged to the Rams' anonymous special teams crew. "The touchdown was the frosting on the cake," defensive tackle Roger Brown said. "The blocked punt was the winner, man."

The lanky Gabriel kept the Packers off balance with 227 passing yards and an effective ground game.

The Rams of course had expected something like this all along. They even expected to block Donny Anderson's punt. Marion Campbell, an assistant coach, sent the stratagem in. It is a system that the Rams, like all pro football teams, work on for a few brief moments each week, just so it will be available in an emergency. Instead of trying to hold up the opposing team at the line of scrimmage in hopes of a long punt runback, they station eight men on the line in gaps between the blockers. In Los Angeles' case, Tony Guillory, a substitute linebacker with good height and speed, plays head to head on the center, and goes

whichever way he feels is open.

"This time I went to my right," Guillory said after the game in a Ram dressing room that was tremulous with joy. "The center's got his head down for the snap, so you get a good jump on him and I got off right with the ball. My assignment on the play is really to draw a block from the fullback, so one of the outside guys can come in free. This time nobody touched me and I came right up the middle."

Guillory hit the ball with the side of his left wrist and it wobbled into the hands of Crabb....

—Tex Maule
December 18, 1967

153

From low in the East end zone seats at Cleveland's Municipal Stadium, Milk Bones rained on the frozen field. The Dawg Pound, a howling pack of fans fiercely loyal to the Browns, was in full attack mode, baying at the Broncos as they prepared to take over inside their own two-yard line. Up 20–13 in the AFC Championship Game, Cleveland was a mere 5:32 away from a Super Bowl appearance at last. The most ardent mutts in the NFL set free their frustrations—and their remaining projectiles. "You could feel things crunching under your feet when you ran," Denver wide receiver Vance Johnson said afterward. "Bones and everything were flying through the air. I've never, ever, seen so many biscuits."

The snow was no longer falling, but flakes still swirled in the wind off Lake Erie. The Browns had just gone ahead on Brian Brennan's twisting 48-yard touchdown catch from Bernie Kosar. After bobbling the ensuing kickoff, the Broncos had 98½ treat-strewn yards to travel—just to draw even. Quarterback John Elway had to huddle Denver amid the kennel's din in the end zone. Across the line, Browns linebacker Clay Mathews clapped the shoulder of nosetackle Bob Golic. "This is it," Mathews said.

Elway had entered the league in 1983 as the No. 1 draft pick out of Stanford, the most heralded rookie quarterback since Joe Namath. He had skill (a heavy hitting outfielder, he had hit .349 with nine home runs and 50 RBIs as a sophomore and was chosen first by the New York Yankees in the 1981 summer draft), good genes (his dad, Jack, was a college coach who favored the pass) and a supersonic right arm (in four years as a starter he had passed for 9,349 yards with a .612 completion percentage, the second-best in school history). But lately, Elway had

Elway's late-game heroics put the Broncos in the Super Bowl and broke the hearts of Cleveland fans everywhere.

Elway completed 22 of 38 passes in spite of a muddy field, a sprained ankle and a hailstorm of dog biscuits.

Nobody in the delirious Cleveland throng could have imagined such a nightmarish turn of events. Browns wide receiver Brian Brennan had just made it 20–13 by twisting safety Dennis Smith into a bow tie on a 48-yard touchdown reception from quarterback Bernie Kosar, a play that seemed destined to go straight into the NFL archives. Super slow motion, voice of doom narrating: "On a frigid afternoon,

a short, curly-haired young Catholic lad from Boston College snatched glory from the ominous skies over Lake Erie and presented it to this desperate city

In SI's Words

of rust and steel...." Brennan was Dwight Clark making "the Catch" against the Dallas Cowboys to send the 49ers on to Super Bowl XVI. He was a

vivid canvas to be placed in the Cleveland Museum of Art. Hell, he was the glue-fingered kid who caught the Hail Mary bomb against the University of Miami in 1984 to earn Doug Flutie a Heisman Trophy, wasn't he? Well, no, that was Gerard Phelan.

Nonetheless, Brennan sure looked to be the hero of the game.

—Rick Telander
January 18, 1987

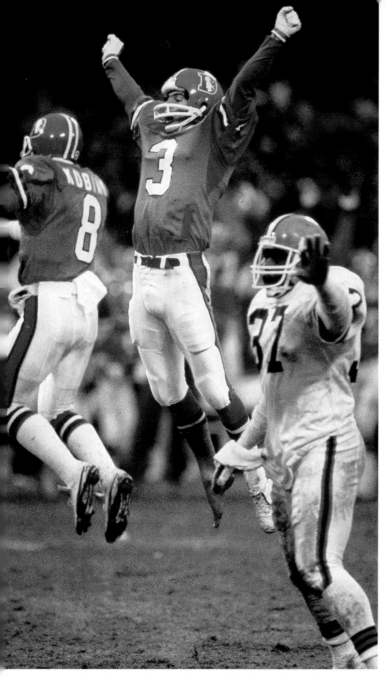

Karlis's 33-yard field goal capped the dramatic win for Denver.

been experiencing more road trouble than a '69 Pinto. Denver had scored only three TDs in the Broncos' last three games of the regular season, and so far at Municipal Stadium, Elway had been able to carry Denver just 216 yards on his sprained left ankle. In his first two fourth-quarter possessions he had advanced the ball only 15 yards.

Now he stood, back pressed against a stand full of frigid Dawg snouts, with little time left and no end zone in sight. The 27-year-old Elway looked around at the Denver offense and smiled. He cracked a joke: "Well, we got these guys right where we want them." He gave a pep talk: "If you work hard, good things are gonna come.

We've got a long way to go, so let's get going." He smiled again. Then he limped to the line of scrimmage and started the Drive.

The Drive began with four touches by running back Sammy Winder, which wedged the ball out to the 15. Breathing room. Elway eluded the Browns' three-man front and scrambled for 11 yards. He got a pass off on the next play, hitting flanker Steve Sewell for 22. Before the two-minute warning, Elway fired to wideout Steve Watson for 12 more yards and a first down on the Cleveland 40.

Cleveland was in a prevent defense with five defensive backs. Safety Ray Ellis almost picked off Elway's next heave at the five, then nose tackle Dave Puzzuoli sacked Elway for an eight-yard loss, twisting his tender left ankle. The rabid fans smelled blood. Facing third-and-18, Denver coach Dan Reeves instructed Elway to get half of the yardage now, the rest on fourth down. Elway almost got none, then got more than enough. Watson, in motion, ran between Elway and the shotgun snap, the ball deflecting off his rear end. Acting quickly, Elway snatched the ball from the turf and fired a 20-yard strike to wideout Mark Jackson. Even the Broncos' screwups were paying off.

Elway threw 14 yards to Sewell. After an incompletion to Watson, Reeves called for a quarterback draw, and Elway hobbled out of bounds at the five. Cleveland's prevent was in peril. In the huddle Elway barked out "Release 66." Jackson slanted into the end zone. Elway fired a rocket. Touchdown. Rich Karlis, barefoot, kicked the extra point, and with 37 seconds to go, the game was tied. "I felt like a baseball catcher," Jackson said. "That was a John Elway fastball, outside and low."

Elway had taken Denver 98 yards in 15 plays by completing six of eight passes for 78 yards and rushing for the other 20. "We shut him down the whole damn game," said Browns defensive end Sam Clancy, "and then in the last two minutes he showed what he was made of."

In overtime, the Browns punted and Elway led what seemed an inevitable victory march—The Overdrive?— completing two passes for 50 yards to set up Karlis's winning 33-yard boot. Just when the Dawgs had nearly sunk their teeth into their first AFC title, Elway had ripped it from their yapping mouths. "In the face of adversity champions are born," Jackson said afterward. Then he smiled. "We have a lot of sayings out in Denver."

Front Cover

Walter Iooss Jr.

Back Cover

Walter Iooss Jr.

Front Matter

Half-title page, John Iacono;
Title page, Walter Iooss Jr.

Introduction

6, Walter Iooss Jr.; 7, Neil Leifer; 8, John D. Hanlon; 9, John W. McDonough; 10, Heinz Kluetmeier; 11, Heinz Kluetmeier.

BIG GAMES

12-13, Walter Iooss Jr.; 14, Walter Iooss Jr.; 15, Neil Leifer; 16, Walter Iooss Jr.; 17, Neil Leifer; 19, Walter Iooss Jr.; 20, James F. Flores/NFL Photos; 21, Vernon J. Biever; 22, Neil Leifer; 24, Walter Iooss Jr.; 25, left, Neil Leifer, right, Walter Iooss Jr.; 26, Hy Peskin; 28, Hy Peskin; 29, Hy Peskin; 31, HOF/NFL Photos; 32, HOF/NFL Photos; 33, AP WWP/NFL Photos; 35, HOF/NFL Photos; 36, HOF/NFL Photos; 37, AP; 39, NFL Photos; 40, AP; 41, UPI/Corbis-Bettmann; 42-43, Heinz Kluetmeier.

ONE-MAN GAMES

44, Heinz Kluetmeier; 45, Walter Iooss Jr.; 46, Heinz Kluetmeier; 47, Tony Triolo; 49, UPI/Corbis-Bettmann; 50-51, UPI/Corbis-Bettmann; 51, UPI/Corbis-Bettmann; 53, UPI/Corbis-Bettmann; 54, left, Vernon J. Biever, right, HOF/NFL Photos; 55, all, HOF/NFL Photos; 57, Lou Witt/NFL Photos; 58, Al Messerschmidt/NFL Photos; 59, Al Messerschmidt/NFl Photos; 61, Vernon J. Biever; 62, Walter Iooss Jr.; 63, Tony Tomsic; 64, Fred Kaplan/NFL Photos; 66, Russ Reed/NFL Photos; 67, Fred Kaplan, NFL Photos; 68, Heinz Kluetmeier; 69, Fred Roe/NFL Photos; 70, Heinz Kluetmeier; 71, John Iacono.

COMEBACKS

72-73, Heinz Kluetmeier; 74, John Biever; 75, Long Photography; 76, UPI/Corbis-Bettmann; 77, Jerry Wachter; 78, John Biever; 80, John Biever; 81, Rick Stewart/Allsport; 82, UPI/Corbis-Bettmann; 84, Russ Reed/NFL Photos; 85, Frank Rippon/NFL Photos; 87, Russ Russell/NFL Photos; 88, UPI/Corbis-Bettmann; 89, Russ Russell, NFL Photos; 91, Heinz Kluetmeier; 92, John Iacono; 93, Jerry Wachter; 94, James F. Flores/NFL Photos; 96, Frank Rippon/NFL Photos; 97, UPI/Corbis-Bettmann.

NAIL-BITERS

98-99, Heinz Kluetmeier; 100, Vernon J. Biever; 101, Damian Strohmeyer; 102, UPI/Corbis-Bettmann; 103, Ronald C. Modra; 105, UPI/Corbis-Bettmann; 106, Vernon J. Biever; 107, UPI/Corbis-Bettmann; 109, Heinz Kluetmeier; 110, Ronald C. Modra; 111, Al Messerschmidt/NFL Photos; 113, Rich Clarkson; 114, left, Rich Clarkson; 114-115, Herb Scharfman; 115, right, Rich Clarkson; 116, UPI/Corbis-Bettmann; 118, top, UPI/Corbis-Bettmann, inset, NFL Photos; 119, NFL Photos; 121, Walter Iooss Jr.; 122, Walter Iooss Jr.; 123, Damian Strohmeyer; 125, George Gellatly/NFL Photos; 126, UPI/Corbis-Bettmann; 127, George Gellatly/NFL Photos.

FANTASTIC FINISHES

128-129, John Biever; 130, Heinz Kluetmeier; 131, Walter Iooss Jr.; 132, John D. Hanlon; 133, John Biever; 134, AP WWP/NFL Photos; 136, John Iacono; 137, NFL Photos; 138, Richard Mackson; 139, Walter Iooss Jr.; 140, Richard Mackson; 141, Walter Iooss Jr.; 142, Heinz Kluetmeier; 144, Heinz Kluetmeier; 145, NFL Photos; 146, John Biever; 148, John Iacono; 149, Jerry Wachter; 151, Walter Iooss Jr.; 152, Neil Leifer; 153, Neil Leifer; 154, John D. Hanlon; 156, John Biever; 157, Richard Mackson.

INDEX

159